BITTER WATER

TO
FINE
WINE

BITTER WATER

TO

FINE WINE

TURNING SETBACKS INTO SETUPS

C. Milton
Grannum, Ph.D.

PUBLICATIONS

Fort Washington, PA 19034

Bitter Water to Fine Wine

Published by CLC Publications

U.S.A.
P.O. Box 1449, Fort Washington, PA 19034
UNITED KINGDOM
CLC International (UK)
Unit 5, Glendale Avenue, Sandycroft, Flintshire, CH5 2QP

© 2019 C. Milton Grannum

All rights reserved. Published 2019

Printed in the United States of America

ISBN (trade paper): 978-1-61958-302-3

ISBN (e-book): 978-1-61958-303-0

Italics in Scripture quotations are the emphasis of the author.

Contents

Author's Preface

This book deals with my spiritual journey, and some of the many difficult situations God has allowed—and continues to allow—in my life. I call these situations "bitter waters," and they can influence, shape, and sometimes frame us. Your own bitter waters may have come through difficulties, persecutions, neglect, defeats, and hindrances you have experienced and may be experiencing even now.

Some of my bitter waters came in the pains of growing up: my childhood, my teenage years, and my young adulthood. At age 14, I was kicked out of my home for my faith. As a teenager, every Saturday I walked to my pastor's home—a twelve-mile round trip—to serve him and his wife, as my tithe to God and His kingdom. I continued to tithe consistently, even as I struggled through four years of Bible college with very little money.

Some of my bitter waters came in the early years my of ministry. When I got married in Philadelphia in 1967, due to limited resources I had to take my bride on our honeymoon to Tennessee on a Greyhound bus. Several years later, my wife and I made the very difficult and painful decision to put all of our savings into helping finance our new congregation. Later on, we decided to sell our home to help purchase the campus now known as New Covenant Church of Philadelphia. This was an extremely hard decision for our entire family.

Through Christ, however, we all have the ability to turn life's bitter waters into wine just as Jesus did in the second chapter of the Gospel of John. In this book, I share stories of how God did this in my life, and how He can do it in your life, too.

Life brings challenging circumstances that tend to put many of us on the spot. We need to develop a committed and stubborn faith that can make hard decisions. If you are really interested in growing and developing a stretching faith to trust God for the difficult, the challenging, and in many cases the impossible, then this book is for you.

I would like to take this opportunity to express profound gratitude to my dear and loving wife, the Rev. Dr. Hyacinth Bobb Grannum, who has encouraged and supported me for over 50 years. Thanks to our children, Dwayne, Gillian, Aubrey, Andrew, and Samuel; to our daughters-in-law, Chivas and Samantha; and to our precious grandchildren, who continue to inspire me.

I would like to thank Apostle Abraham Fenton and his dear wife, Dr. Eva Fenton, for their wisdom, support, and partnership in the founding of the New Covenant Church of Philadelphia and for their ongoing friendship over the decades. My wife and I are sincerely and significantly indebted it to them.

Finally, special thanks to our church's ministry administrator, Miss Wangui Mwangi, whose commitment, discipline, organizing, and editing skills helped me to complete this book.

I'm Growing

I'm growing as I'm learning, as I'm
feeling, as I'm listening.
I'm growing as I'm risking, as I'm falling, as I'm rising.
I'm growing as I'm holding on, and learning to let go.

I'm growing as I'm perceiving, as I'm
giving, as I'm receiving.
I'm growing as I'm believing, as I'm loving, as I'm caring.
I'm growing as I'm holding on, and finally—letting go.

I'm growing as I'm moving just past knowing who I am
I'm growing as I'm discovering who I really can become.
As I'm reaching, as I'm stretching
far beyond my usual self,
I'm growing as I'm becoming closer
to my intended self.
—C. Milton Grannum

Introduction

To a certain extent, we all experience some kind of suffering and need help to survive. Over the decades as a student of the Scriptures and a pastor, I have been on a stimulating journey seeking to accurately identify and properly interpret the many pieces and stages of my life, and use them for God's glory. I have sought to create meaning out of pain, perspective out of rejection, and fine wine out of very bitter waters.

The apostle Paul states, "If what was built on the foundation survives the fire, the builder will receive a reward" (1 Cor. 3:14, GNT). In the light of that, how does one use a variety of negative experiences and turn them into the fine wine of eternal significance?

Significance, like the making of fine wine, is all a matter of time. Experiences that are forgotten, rejected, disregarded, or wasted are of little significance. What is remembered, properly interpreted, reconstructed and effectively used for eternity, becomes of great significance. Paul wrote to Timothy,

Significance, like the making of fine wine, is all a matter of time.

"Discipline yourself for the purpose of godliness . . . since it holds promise for the present life and also for the life to come" (1 Timothy 4:7–8, NASB). I continue to be intrigued by the interesting story found in John chapter 2 in the Bible, about Jesus and His mother, Mary.

Let's read the story in John 2:1–11.

> On the third day there was a wedding at Cana in Galilee, and the mother of Jesus was there. Jesus also was invited to the wedding with his disciples. When the wine ran out, the mother of Jesus said to him, "They have no wine." And Jesus said to her, "Woman, what does this have to do with me? My hour has not yet come." His mother said to the servants, "Do whatever he tells you."
>
> Now there were six stone water jars there for the Jewish rites of purification, each holding twenty or thirty gallons. Jesus said to the servants, "Fill the jars with water." And they filled them up to the brim. And he said to them, "Now draw some out and take it to the master of the feast." So they took it. When the master of the feast tasted the water now become wine, and did not know where it came from (though the servants who had drawn the water knew), the master of the

feast called the bridegroom and said to him,
"Everyone serves the good wine first, and
when people have drunk freely, then the poor
wine. But you have kept the good wine until
now." This, the first of his signs, Jesus did at
Cana in Galilee, and manifested his glory.
And his disciples believed in him.

When Jesus, His mother, Mary, and His twelve disciples attended a wedding in Cana of Galilee, the wine ran out. Why was the shortage of wine (a potentially embarrassing situation for the newly married couple) brought to Mary's attention? Possibly Mary was related to either the bride or the groom. In any case, Mary in turn brought the shortage to Jesus' attention. Jesus' initial response highlights two things:

1. He did not think or feel that the shortage of wine was really His concern.
2. He did not think or feel that this was His time for revealing Himself and openly pursuing certain aspects of His anointing and His ministry (i.e., performing a miracle).

In spite of Jesus' response, and right within His hearing, Mary instructed the servants to do whatever Jesus directed them to do. Being put on the spot, Jesus instructed the servants to fill six large stone jars with water, and then to pour out some of the water and to serve it to the master of the feast. When the master of the feast drank the water (now turned to wine), he was shocked and surprised, and told the bridegroom, "You've saved the best wine for last!"

Interestingly, though up to this point His disciples had been selected and had left much to follow Him, it was only after they experienced this miracle that the Bible says, "his disciples believed in him."

Turning water into wine was His first visible miracle and divine operation. The significant insight is that Jesus' first miracle and supernatural act came as He sought to address a simple human need and concern (saving the bridegroom from social embarrassment). This was the beginning of His ministry, and His mother Mary helped Him to make this happen.

Life confronts you and me with many different experiences, many kinds of waters. Some are pleasant, some not; some are clear, some muddy; some are joyful, some painful; some are sweet, some bitter. How we address these many different waters definitely influences the quality of our lives and the effectiveness of our leadership.

The passage describes how Jesus turned water into wine at the urging of His mother. It shows that He had someone in His life—Mary—who believed in Him, His calling, His anointing, His potential, and His future. It was her pushing Him to act in a very unusual situation that enabled the very disciples He had selected and were following Him to really believe in Him. She also pushed Him beyond what was then His present paradigm and self-perception.

Everybody wants to become something, to accomplish something, but sometimes we just need someone to give us a little push. Mary, the mother of Jesus, propelled Jesus into His hour when she pushed Him to address the shortage of wine at a wedding in Cana.

Everybody wants to become something, to accomplish something, but sometimes we just need someone to give us a little push.

I relate this story to the many life-impacting experiences in my journey and how God used all of them to push my family and me into our present hour. Indeed, anyone can cooperate with God and allow Him to turn all our setbacks into setups. As we actively pursue the possibilities and opportunities of God's preordained destiny for us, we will always have to pay a price, but it will be worth it.

You and I have a series of big decisions to make. As we look at our lives, it is easy to focus simply on the shortages, the challenges, the perceived inadequacies, the disappointments, and the many negative experiences. We must reject the emotional urge to allow our past experiences to push us into spending our lives living with and wallowing in painful memories and bitter waters.

The foundational illustration of this book is the Wedding at Cana story found in the book of John, chapter 2 when Jesus and His disciples attended a wedding ceremony and experienced a critical need that required immediate attention—they ran out of wine during the reception. When provided with this information Mary, the mother of Jesus, told Jesus and asked him to do something about it. The way in which Jesus handled this need has given me significant insights in my spiritual growth. You will find many reflections of the story in this book and prayerfully you will be pushed to a quality of thought and action necessary for the fulfillment of your needs and the needs around you.

It is my hope that, through the vignettes of my life in the chapters that follow, you will gain insight in how you, too, can overcome difficult situations and fulfill your life's purpose.

Wisdom for Living

1. Who are some of the people who helped to discover and to empower you?
2. What were some of your first reactions when they were pushing you?
3. As you look back at your life, what are some of the things for which you are most grateful?

Chapter 1

My Early Life:
Very Bitter Water

I was born into an impoverished home in what was then British Guiana, the only British-controlled and English-speaking country in South America. (Today, it is known as Guyana.) My father did not live with us and was never there for us. I remember getting a full glass of milk only once a year at Christmas and a whole egg only on my birthday.

For the first fourteen years of my life, I slept on the floor of our house each night. Some time ago, I was visiting two of my brothers in the living room of one of their homes. As we sat there reminiscing, we suddenly came to the realization that the living room we were sitting in was bigger than the entire house in which our family of seven lived.

*For the first fourteen years of my life, I
slept on the floor of our house each night.*

I was just ten years old when the Missionary Board of the Church of God in Anderson, Indiana, sent the Rev. Herman Smith and his beautiful wife, Mrs. Lavera Smith,[1] to be long-term missionaries in what was then British Guiana, the only British controlled and English-speaking country in South America. It is presently known as Guyana. Before their arrival, the Rev. George Jeffrey, the strong national leader who had affiliated his work with the Church of God in Anderson Indiana, had passed away. The Smiths moved very quickly in establishing new outreaches of the Church of God in the country.

Guyana is divided into three counties; Essequibo, Demerara, and Berbice. Its population is made up of six main ethnic groups: Amerindians, Africans, Indians, Europeans, Portuguese, and Chinese. As there were already churches in the county of Demerara where the capital city Georgetown is located, the Smiths moved sought to develop congregations in the other counties as well. Many Indian families in the the Corentyne District[2] of the Berbice County of the country are descendants of indentured laborers from India and are practicing Hindis. An outstanding member of their community, Ramalingum Armogum, was converted to Jesus Christ. He was discipled by Pastor Smith, became a Christian leader, and pioneered several congregations in his community.

Seeing the Need and Doing It Right

In the city of Georgetown,[3] where I lived, the Smiths found an old dilapidated building that the Rev. George Jeffrey had erected several decades earlier as a church and home for the aged at Bel Air Street, in the Albouystown southwest section of the city. The residents had since moved and abandoned the building. I was among the many little boys who regularly threw rocks through the already broken and glassless windows so as to watch the dozens of bats fly out. I'm sure when the Smiths first saw this building, they wondered if anything good could come out of this. I am struck by how their subsequent restoration of the building exemplified how they seized the opportunity to turn very, very bitter waters into wine.

The couple immediately focused on the community's children and youth. Their strategy was to create and empower capable young people for God's kingdom—to reach children, lead them to a life-changing walk with Jesus Christ, and train them to be responsible young people who would later become leaders and establish families in the church. With this in mind, they did an assessment, organized quickly, and built a new multiroom facility that became the first church in the entire country with Sunday school rooms for each children's age group.

Their strategy was to create and empower capable young people for God's kingdom.

After building the new church, the Smiths expertly planned the nation's first vacation Bible school (VBS). That August, hundreds of children from that poor neighborhood gathered to attend something they had never experienced before. Since all the children were on vacation from school, it was a tremendous opportunity to lead them to the Lord.

Touched by the Ministry of Love

At age eleven, I was attending a Roman Catholic school in the city of Georgetown. My entire family was Roman Catholic, and from the catechism I knew that attending a non-Catholic church was a mortal sin. Of course, there were varieties of sins, but a mortal sin was a big one, and without an act of confession to the priest, it could cause you to end up in hell.

I remember that bright, sunny summer morning when the newly renovated Church of God held the first VBS session. The church heavily marketed the event to the community months before using flyers, posters, banners, and door-to-door visitation. As a result, hundreds of children showed up for this brand-new experience.

And yet, I was totally unaware that the church building had been renovated or that a new congregation had begun in the community. I knew nothing about this new event called "vacation Bible school." I simply happened to be at home one day when I heard the singing of children and the playing of music on the street.

Naturally, I ran out to see what was happening, and to my surprise, hundreds of children and a number of adults were marching, singing, handing out flyers and balloons, and inviting neighborhood children to follow the group to a fun time. I followed the procession that led right to the church. Everyone went in—except me. I stood outside, thinking that it seemed to be so much fun. Everyone seemed to be excited, and two adults, apparently teachers, kept inviting me to come in.

As I stood outside the church, terrified to go in (as I said before, my Catholic catechism had taught me it was a mortal sin to enter a Protestant church), I could hear them reciting Bible verses and singing the song,

Jesus loves the little children,
All the children of the world.
Red and yellow, black and white.
All are precious in His sight.
Jesus loves the little children of the world.

Two days later, Pastor Smith and the teachers organized the children to again march around the streets of my neighborhood, singing songs. Imagine hundreds of children walking through the streets with music and flyers, inviting others to join the procession.

Despite my reluctance, I wanted to find out why these children were so happy and having so much fun. Slowly and hesitantly, I joined the procession and found myself marching with the group to the church building and into the room assigned to my age group (nine-to-twelve-year-olds). As I entered the building, I convinced myself that if my priest found out about my participation, I would just tell him, "Father, I was with the children, and I was pushed into the building."

The VBS sessions ran from 9 a.m. to noon and included learning new songs and memorizing scriptures, which I thoroughly enjoyed. It was a fascinating experience and the longest children's event that I had ever participated in. This became the beginning of a sequence of experiences that transformed my life.

"Come and Be My Helper"

Two days later I was excitedly participating in arts and crafts. I clearly remember how the event provided everything needed to capture the interest of the children. Each child had a task including artwork, picture painting, short Bible stories to read, and things to draw. For children living in poor conditions, VBS was the greatest treat ever—absolutely the most fun time I had ever experienced in my life.

That day there must have been fifty to sixty children in my classroom. After I had completed my activity, Pastor Smith asked me what I was doing. When I told him nothing, he made a request that was life-changing to me: "If you have finished your artwork, why don't you come and be my helper and help the other children?"

Come and be my helper. There are not enough words to express the significance of that request. Imagine this pastor (an imposing man, towering over six feet tall and weighing close to 270 pounds) inviting me, a Roman Catholic child who wasn't even supposed to be there, to be his helper! While I was not quite sure what he had in mind, I was in awe that he wanted me to be his "helper" after only knowing me for two days. Wow!

Wisdom for Living

1. What would you imagine would be the future of a child who got a full glass of milk only once a year at Christmas, a whole egg only on his birthday, and who slept on the floor the first fourteen years of his life?
2. What do you think were some of the advantages gained by the Smiths in building the first church in

the country with separate classrooms for each Sunday school age group?

3. I was just eleven years old when the pastor said to me, "Why don't you come and be my helper?" If you were in my shoes, what thoughts would have gone through your mind?

4. What did the pastor's request to me reveal about his philosophy of ministry?

5. Why do you think the pastor was interested in being one of the teachers who worked with children ages nine to twelve?

Chapter 2

The Greatest Sermon
I Ever Saw

I awoke the following day with tremendous excitement and immediately begin preparing to get back to vacation Bible school, where I was the pastor's helper. Though I was still a poor, barefooted boy who wore what we called "house clothes," I felt different. I had been affirmed and felt like I was somebody very special.

Then, three days later in VBS class, a boy wearing shoes stepped on my foot. Angrily and in pain, I said to him, "Pick up the thing you just stepped on." I really wanted him to recognize and acknowledge that he had stepped on my foot. When he just looked at me and turned away, I followed him, commanding, "Pick up the thing you just stepped on."

Then, right there in the classroom of close to 60 children, we began to fight, diverting all the children's attention to us. Pastor Smith immediately rushed towards us. Before we knew it, he had lifted us both by the seat of our pants, carried us outside, and lowered us onto the grass.

Although my opponent wanted to continue fighting, I was too embarrassed to do so. The boy began cursing and eventually left. I remained sitting on the grass contemplating my future. After only a few days of being promoted to pastor's helper, I was sure that I was about to be put out of VBS. Furthermore, I feared the beating I would endure when I returned home if my mother caught wind of my fight. I was in a fix. As I sat there with my head resting on my knees, I heard loud footsteps on the sidewalk coming toward me. It was the pastor.

"Where is the other boy?" he asked. I answered, "Sir, he was here cursing and wanting to fight; then he left."

To my surprise, the pastor said, "I have come out to get you. I want you to come back in with me."

I was awestruck. I could not believe that he had left a room full of well-behaved children just to invite me back into the classroom. What redemption! What forgiveness! What restoration for an eleven-year-old child! Filled with gratitude, I got up and went into that building with him; I have been connected to that church, the Church of God, Anderson, Indiana, and to that pastor's family, ever since.

> *To my surprise, the pastor said,*
> *"I have come out to get you."*

For over six decades, I have declared that I did not give my heart to Jesus based on the great sermons I had heard. I finally gave my heart and life to Jesus because of the sermon I experienced when my pastor left all the children in that classroom to personally take me back in. What a sermon! It made me more than just a church member or attender. It motivated and empowered me to become involved in the life of the church.

After VBS, I became active as a leader in youth ministries and a Sunday school teacher. I also was part of a group of teenagers who led regular cottage meetings and many evangelistic programs in the church. I believe that my pastor and his wife, and many of the adult leaders, encouraged, befriended, and nurtured me and other children because they saw that we had hearts for God.

Genuine conversion may or may not result from some exciting or emotional experience. There are times when people come to Christ in a dramatic encounter, such as Paul on the Damascus Road. Mine came because of a pastor left a classroom of children in search of just one eleven-year-old boy. In that solitary encounter, I saw, felt, and experienced the forgiveness and love of God. As a result, I committed both my heart and life to Christ.

My pastor's compassion was a classic illustration and reflection of the sovereign, unmerited favor and love of God. He and his wife had a commitment to children that significantly influenced my approach to children in ministry. In my current pastorate, I have over twenty young assistants, most of whom are under twelve years old.

This program began when Jerad Werts (nine years old at the time) approached me with a request to help in the church.

*In that solitary encounter, I
saw, felt and experienced the
forgiveness and love of God.*

He asked if he could help paint speed bumps on our campus.
That one request paved the way for a full-fledged leadership
development program open to all children, regardless of their
membership status. Through this program, we seek to train
and equip children and youth to develop into outstanding
Christian leaders and role models in their family and community. Participants learn the importance of faith, integrity,
respect for self and others, humility, and self-discipline.

Christ used this approach when He called, connected with,
developed, and sent His disciples into the world to actively
pursue His mission. In the same way, my pastor and his wife
came and joined themselves to us. They created a ministry
that connected children, youth, and adults to each other and
to them—and, ultimately, to God.

Why do I consider the principle of connection as my most
important leadership lesson? Because everybody needs somebody to help them become the person God intended them
to be. We cannot discover or become our best selves all by
ourselves. This is why the church is considered a *fellowship*,
which means people in relationships, first with God and then
with one another.

True leadership involves a series of connections. From the
very beginning of Jesus' leadership He chose to make connections with individuals. He saw them as children connected
to a father, as friends connected to one another and as sheep

connected to a shepherd. Effective and life-changing impartation requires meaningful relationships and vulnerability.

Now, after over six decades, when I think of my pastor saying, "Come and be my helper" and "I have come out to get you, come back in with me," I cannot help but think of Paul's second letter to Timothy, where he says, "Only Luke is with me. Get Mark and bring him with you because he is helpful to me in my ministry" (4:11). This is a significant statement, because Paul had previously rejected Mark for ministry.

True leadership involves a
series of connections.

Part of Mark's story is found in Acts 12:25, 13:2–14, and 15:35–16:3. Paul and Barnabas were ministering in Salamis and John Mark (referred to as Mark) was their assistant. As they traveled to Paphos, John Mark departed from them. Later on in ministry, Barnabas sought to invite John Mark to minister with them again, but Paul rejected the idea, since to him, Mark was a failure. It is interesting that in Second Timothy 4:1 Paul asks for John Mark's help, and now sees him as valuable for the ministry. Mark, a perceived failure, is restored, and Paul, an apostle, has matured!

Paul and Mark's connection did not start off well, yet even though it took time, it ended well, with both fulfilling their purposes. Likewise, my pastor's impression of me (fighting with another boy) was not very good, but he took the time to connect with me, and that resulted in me fulfilling my purpose.

Because of this experience, I can identify with the Edgar A. Guest[4] poem "I'd Rather See A Sermon Than Hear One Any Day":

I'd rather see a sermon
than hear one any day;
I'd rather one should walk with me
than merely tell the way.

The eye's a better pupil
and more willing than the ear,
Fine counsel is confusing,
but example's always clear;

And the best of all preachers
are the men who live their creeds,
For to see good put in action
is what everybody needs.

I soon can learn to do it
if you'll let me see it done;
I can watch your hands in action,
but your tongue too fast may run.

And the lecture you deliver
may be very wise and true,
But I'd rather get my lessons
by observing what you do;

> For I might misunderstand you
>   and the high advice you give,
> But there's no misunderstanding
>   how you act and how you live.[5]

Wisdom for Living

1. How would you have felt if you had a negative situation in church and was put out?
2. Why did I remain sitting on the grass with my head bowed?
3. What do you think the pastor saw when he looked out the door and saw me sitting there?
4. What are some of the great sermons you can remember having experienced in your life?
5. What is the message of Edgar A. Guest's poem?
6. What is the significance of Jesus coming to earth and seeking to connect Himself to us?
7. Why is the principle of connecting so significant in the life and effectiveness of a local church? Why are two better than one?

Chapter 3

The Gift of Initiative

The first question which the priest and the Levite asked was, "If I stop to help this man, what will happen to me?" But . . . the good Samaritan reversed the question: "If I do not stop to help this man, what will happen to him?"

—Rev. Dr. Martin Luther King, Jr.

I cannot remember a time in my life when I did not feel that God was with me. Even as a child attending a Roman Catholic school, I sensed God's call on my life. This made it easy and natural for me to become actively involved in the church.

My first sense of God's call on my life occurred early in childhood, when I began attending Sunday school at our next-door neighbor's home. As I heard the stories about Jesus and His disciples, I knew that I wanted to follow in his footsteps. According to my mother and brothers, I would often say, "When I grow up, I want to be a 'fitherman'—you know, a 'fitherman' like Peter." What I meant to say was "fisherman." Although I could not pronounce the word, I already knew I would one day become a pastor. Each Sunday we sang children's songs, and my favorite went like this:

A fisherman I will be.
A fisherman I will be.
I will catch much fish for Jesus
Upon the wide blue sea.

The Gift of Bold Ideas

As I contemplate my life, I realize that God has consistently given me ideas that have resulted in great moral strength and soul courage. For example, as a youngster, I recall hearing church people preaching on the streets, so I ran home and began preaching to empty soda bottles I had lined up. I even remember trying to teach the bottles the Lord's Prayer!

After VBS and other church-related experiences, I got this burning idea I could not wait to share with my Sunday school teacher—that I believed God wanted me to teach a Sunday school class. When I finally got up the courage to tell her this, she asked, "What did you say?"

I believed God wanted me to teach a Sunday school class.

"I believe that God wants me to teach a class. I have learned ten songs and ten verses from the Bible in VBS, and I know children who don't know them."

After a moment of contemplation she finally said, "You know, we don't have children teaching classes, and furthermore, I don't think that Brother Smith would allow that." I heard her, but I was not satisfied with her response. If the pastor didn't want me to teach, he would have to tell that to me himself, because I believed that God was calling me to teach a class.

Later, when I saw the pastor was alone, I looked up at this nearly 270-pound giant and said, "Brother Smith, I believe that God is calling me to teach a Sunday school class."

"What did you say?" he asked.

It felt like a David and Goliath situation.[6] He repeated with his deep bass voice, "What did you say?" I restated, "I believe that God is calling me to teach a Sunday school class. I attended VBS, I've learned ten Scripture passages and ten songs, and there are kids on my street who didn't come to VBS and don't know those songs and verses."

He stood there and looked at me and thought for a long, long while. Then, suddenly, without notice, he said, "Okay. Do you see this front bench? That's your bench. Bring the kids and teach them."

Wow! That was all I wanted to hear. At eleven-and-a-half years old and with little biblical education, I had already learned a very significant lesson—share your ideas and speak up! If no one else listens, God does.

I think about the boy Samuel in the Bible. First Samuel 2:18–20 states,

> Samuel was ministering before the LORD, a boy clothed with a linen ephod. And his mother used to make for him a little robe and take it to him each year when she went up with her husband to offer the yearly sacrifice. Then Eli would bless Elkanah and his wife, and say, "May the LORD give you children by this woman for the petition she asked of the LORD." So then they would return to their home.

Verse 26 reads, "Now the boy Samuel continued to grow both in stature and in favor with the LORD and also with man."

Much of Samuel's development is attributable to Eli. He discerned young Samuel's heart and gave him opportunities to serve in the temple. He understood the importance of creating an environment conducive to developing a child's potential. The reason I approached my pastor with a novel idea was not only due to the gift of ideas that God had given me. It was also because my pastor and his wife had created a caring and loving environment that helped children *want* to participate in ministry. Because of this, I discovered my teaching gift and honed my skills. I have been teaching for over sixty years.

The Bicycle Experience in Leadership

I remember how my brother taught me to ride a bike. He would run behind me and hold the bike to support me as I learned to peddle and balance myself. When he let go without my knowledge, I didn't fall until I realized that he had let go. The more he taught me, the more proficient I became, and the more confident I felt.

The way my brother taught me to ride a bike is much like how my pastor gave me the opportunity to lead by creating and teaching my own class. The risk my pastor took on me became the "bicycle experience" in my leadership development path. Today, I use this illustration in leadership training to show that anyone can lead if he or she

1. has the desire.
2. is willing to be led.
3. is willing to submit to the leadership methods and strategy of others.
4. takes the first step in self-preparation.
5. is prepared to submit to the leadership and guidance of the Holy Spirit.

The Power of Initiative

Think of that important thing you want to achieve. Visualize it as having been accomplished. Imagine yourself basking in the satisfaction of a job well done. What does it look like? What does it taste like? What does it feel like? The only way you will experience the joy, beauty, and fulfillment that come by achieving one's goals is if you intentionally use your personal initiative.

> *The way my brother taught me to ride*
> *a bike is much like how my pastor*
> *gave me the opportunity to lead.*

Personal Initiative

In his blog, Todd Smith makes a strong argument for the power of personal initiative.

> What is personal initiative? Dwight Turner, a newspaper columnist, defines it this way: "Initiative is a force of personal energy that arises from deep within and flows forth into positive, goal-oriented action."
>
> Your personal initiative is your inner power that starts all action. It is the enemy of procrastination or self-doubt. It's the spark that creates your productive efforts and success.[7]

How, then, does one achieve success? Smith quotes Napoleon Hill as saying, "Success is something you must achieve without someone telling you what to do or why you should do it." In other words, Smith says, "Success comes to those who are proactive.... No one told Fred Smith to start FedEx; he started it using his own personal initiative. No one encouraged Sergey Brin and Larry Page to start Google. They did it using their own personal initiative."[8] Success and achievement require daily decisions that go beyond the norm and consistently use one's initiative that allows one to achieve.

Long ago I reached the conclusion that having the gift of initiative is only the beginning to a life of power and purpose. Only those who utilize it ever experience the full satisfaction of achieving their life-long goals. The gift of initiative is a result of discovering and utilizing our talents and abilities. These gifts, talents, and abilities are an investment God made in us. They are parts of His strengths and also reflect His design and direction for our journey on earth.

The Old Testament story of Nehemiah clearly demonstrates that initiative is indeed an essential quality of leadership. Nehemiah was a man who knew how to utilize his leadership skills at the right moment to create victories. He remains one of the great leaders and managers in the history of the Bible.

> *The gift of initiative is a result*
> *of discovering and utilizing*
> *our talents and abilities.*

Nehemiah 2:17–18 indicates that Jerusalem was in trouble. The city was in ruins. Its gates had been destroyed by fire and the city was a disgrace. Upon hearing this, Nehemiah used his access to the king to get authorization to help rebuild the city . This is shown in Nehemiah 2:4–5, which reads, "Then the king said to me, 'What are you requesting?' So I prayed to the God of heaven. And I said to the king, 'If it pleases the king, and if your servant has found favor in your sight, that you send me to Judah, to the city of my fathers' graves, that I may rebuild it.'"

Upon arriving in Jerusalem, he shared his vision with the people, then mobilized and organized them to rebuild the walls, restore the city, and end the national disgrace. Nehemiah utilized the power of initiative so effectively that it took him and the people only fifty-two days to rebuild the entire wall around the city of Jerusalem.

People with initiative see a clear vision, seek a solution to the problems, seek wisdom and counsel, influence others with great ideas, motivate, organize and mobilize, take risks, make and admit mistakes, then follow through to get the mission done.

Wisdom for Living

1. What initiative did I take about my feeling that God was calling me to teach a class?
2. How do you believe I felt when my Sunday school teacher said she did not think that my teaching a class at my age was possible or would be allowed?
3. What do you think motivated me at that young age to personally approach the pastor in spite of what I was told by my Sunday school teacher?
4. What lessons can we learn from the encounters with my Sunday school teacher and pastor?
5. How would you have handled the encounters described in this chapter?
6. How do you think those experiences contributed to my later development, initiative, and leadership?

Chapter 4

Homeless at Age Fourteen

I was fourteen years old and experiencing two lives: a type of heaven at church, and a form of hell at home. For several weeks before I was thrust into a life-impacting change, I had joyful and fulfilling experiences on the one hand, and profoundly hellish, worrying, and threatening experiences on the other.

At church I was involved in serving and working with people and encountering God in profound ways. At home, I was enduring and persevering through unbelievable rejection, abuse, and ridicule because of my commitment of time to God and His church.

Over the previous year, my mother had begun to be very unhappy about my going to the Church of God. My being involved in the "right" church, where I could get a good education and a good job later on, was her major concern, and it was not entirely unjustified. (At that time in our country, most schools were government funded but owned and run by churches and denominations.) She would often say to me, "That church has nothing to offer you. It has no schools, no jobs." In her estimation, only the big churches—Roman Catholic, Methodist, Presbyterian, Lutheran, and Anglican—had the connections that could ensure me a good job and a solid future.

My mother's early hardships apparently influenced her thinking. The eldest of five children, she was just ten years old when her mother died unexpectedly, leaving her with four siblings and no father in the home. The children had to go and live with their aunt, the matron in charge of female inmates at the Georgetown Guyana prison. They lived in a prison-provided residence within the compound.

Before she turned eleven, she had to quit school to help care for her siblings as well as the children of her aunt. Her tasks involved cleaning the house, going to the market, preparing meals, and doing laundry by hand for the entire household.

Many times while growing up, my mother found life not merely hard and challenging but, in her own words, "actual hell." Her aunt had developed a rough and harsh style of dealing with unruly women prisoners, and she carried that abusive manner home with her. Her approach to child-rearing was a "word and a blow"—physical and verbal abuse. My brothers and I can testify to the fact that her aunt's methods became my mother's style as well. She brought us up the way she had experienced life, leaving each of my four brothers with his own tale to tell.

As a result, my early teen years were the beginning of significant challenges for me at home. I had settled and reconciled in my mind that I would go to church and participate in all the activities on Sundays—only to return home to receive a beating. I would go to Sunday school and the morning service, followed by ministry with a youth evangelistic team at two different institutions for the poor, the sick, and the needy. At 6 p.m., we were back at church for youth fellowship, followed by the evening service.

> *I would go to church and participate*
> *in all the activities on Sundays—*
> *only to return home to receive a beating.*

When I returned home, slaps on my face and lashes on my back were a regular ritual, and I was accustomed to the routine. It is ironic that the giving of my life, not just my heart, resulted in a significantly abusive period in my life.

One Sunday night, while leading the youth fellowship, I was told that my brother was outside looking for me. When I went out, he beat me in the churchyard in the presence of the other youth fellowship members. I was accustomed to such abuse at home, but on that particular night, with my friends watching, the whole experience felt a hundred times more painful. So I ran away—not as much from my brother's blows as from the embarrassment and humiliation. My well-kept secret was now common knowledge among all my friends.

When I look back at my mother's attitude toward "that church," I realize what deep regrets she had at being robbed of an opportunity for an education. If she been able to remain in school and acquire an adequate education, she would have accomplished more and experienced greater self-fulfillment. I believe the anger and abuse I received from her was her misguided way of trying to protect me from a similar fate. She honestly felt I was wasting my efforts in a church that would never help me get a good education, a good job, and, ultimately, a secure future.

Fourteen Years Old and Homeless

For some months, as my mother continued to express her disapproval at my involvement in the Church of God, I felt that something was brewing and about to boil over. I was torn between my family and the church, fearfully struggling to deal with the constant threats and physical abuse.

My mother's determination that I make what she called the "right" decision was based on her concern for my future. However, simply attending a church so that I could eventually get a good job was never my focus. Long before I even knew how to speak well, I knew I wanted to become a fisherman like Peter—and God was fulfilling my dream through my involvement in the church and the mentoring I received from the pastor and other leaders. My mother was not only asking me to give up the personal, social, emotional, and spiritual growth I was experiencing by being part of that fellowship, she was asking me to give up my life's calling.

It was a Sunday morning, and I was preparing for Sunday school and church when the thing that I had been anticipating happened: my mother put me out of our home. She threw all my things outside and told me to go live at the church.

I picked up the few meager possessions she had thrown out, including my school uniform and my school books, then crept back into the house to get the last two significant things I needed: my Bible and my hymnal. I placed all these things in a pillowcase and left that day with nothing else but faith in God.

> ## *She threw all my things outside and told me to go live at the church.*

In the city of Georgetown where I lived, when you walked down the streets, you would see people with all their possessions in a large bag. We called them, "bag people." On that day, at fourteen years old, I became a "bag person."

I remember walking and walking, with no clue as to what I was going to do. I finally thought of going to the home of my Sunday school teacher, Sister Winifred Wilson. I knew that at that time of the morning she would be at church, so I had to wait until Sunday school and morning service were finished before she returned home. I positioned myself on the grass along the route I knew she would use to get home so that I wouldn't miss her. Even today, I can still see myself, sitting on the grass and singing Hymn #364 from my green hymnal:

> Jesus, I my cross have taken,
>   All to leave and follow Thee;
> Destitute, despised, forsaken,
> Thou, from hence, my all shall be.
>   Perish every fond ambition,
> All I've sought or hoped or known;
>   Yet how rich is my condition;

God and heaven are still my own!
Let the world despise and leave me,
They have left my Savior, too;
Human hearts and looks deceive me,
Thou art not, like man, untrue.
And while Thou shalt smile upon me,
God of wisdom, love, and might,
Foes may hate, and friends may shun me:
Show Thy face, and all is bright.
(Henry, Francis Lyte, 1825)[9]

I sang this and other hymns to encourage my spirit as I waited for Sister Wilson. When I finally connected with her, she took me to my pastor, who allowed me to stay at his home for some time. He was an American missionary and proved to be more than just a leader or a religious figure. He and his wife showed me the love of God.

I had stepped out in faith to pursue God's call on my life, and in spite of Satan's plans, God still gets the glory to this day. From age fourteen, my pastor set me up in the home of a godly family, made financial arrangements for my living expenses, and paid my tuition to a private high school. He also helped me significantly during my years of Bible college.

Each morning, while riding my bicycle to school, I would remind myself of the story of David in First Samuel 30:1–6. David and his men went off to war and returned to their home in Ziklag only to discover that their enemies had invaded it, burned down their houses, killed all their cattle, and taken their wives and children captive. David and his men wept uncontrollably.

I had stepped out in faith to pursue God's call on my life

David was greatly distressed, for his men spoke of stoning him. However, the Bible says, "David strengthened himself in the Lord his God" (v. 6). At the tender age of fourteen, I also had to learn to encourage myself in the Lord. Each morning I quoted from Romans 8:35–39:

> Who shall separate us from the love of Christ? Shall tribulation, or distress, or persecution, or famine, or nakedness, or danger, or sword? As it is written, "For your sake we are being killed all the day long; we are regarded as sheep to be slaughtered." No, in all these things we are more than conquerors through him who loved us. For I am sure that neither death nor life, nor angels nor rulers, nor things present nor things to come, nor powers, nor height nor depth, nor anything else in all creation, will be able to separate us from the love of God in Christ Jesus our Lord.

Wisdom for Living

1. How do you think my mother's early experiences of hardship influenced her thinking into adulthood? How have your own childhood experiences influenced you?

2. How do you think my mother's early experiences living with her aunt in a prison compound influenced her self-image and her motherhood?
3. How would you have responded had your mother been opposed to God and to your participation in church?
4. What do you think were some of my fears and feelings when I was put out of my home at age fourteen?
5. What do you think is involved in encouraging oneself in the Lord?

Chapter 5

How Jesus Discovered
a New Dimension
of His Ministry

*There are only two ways to live your life. One
is as though nothing is a miracle. The other is as
though everything is a miracle.*[10]

—Albert Einstein

C reative and productive living involves continually
having new eye-opening and life-impacting experiences that really surprise us. Life teaches us that every
day brings challenges that can become great opportunities for

growth and meaningful self-discoveries. We should never rely on the unlikelihood of problems, challenges, and enemies confronting us, but on our readiness to encounter them with wisdom, knowing that we have spiritual resources at our disposal.

The story about the wedding in Cana depicts how Mary, faced with a major problem, used it to push Jesus beyond His earthly life experiences to that point.

Let's return to the story in John 2:1–11, where Jesus turns water into wine. The location of the wedding—Cana of Galilee—had no social prominence in its day. (In fact, it took biblical scholars 1,800 years before they figured out just where this town was!) Jewish wedding tradition at that time dictated that there would be a time of feasting, followed by the actual wedding ceremony later in the evening.

Sometime during the feast, Mary's attention was drawn to a challenging, surprising, and potentially embarrassing piece of information—they had run out of wine.

Without any more details, the story goes on to say that Mary went directly to Jesus about it. What did she think He could do about the situation? It appears that she was expecting Him to perform a miracle, but since He had not performed any miracles to this point (2:11), why would she expect that?

The answer does not seem hard to find. This is quite in harmony with the mother's hopes, even without any previous miracle on which to base them. Remember, for many long years she had kept in her heart Jesus' words and deeds (Luke 2:51). She must have heard of John the Baptist's witness, of the events of the baptism six weeks earlier, and on that very day every hope must have begun to turn into new life.

Jesus' response when Mary informed Him of the lack of wine is both interesting and fascinating: "Woman, what does this have to do with me? My hour has not yet come" (John 2:4). Mary's reaction was just as fascinating. Standing there with Jesus, she said to the servants, "Do whatever he tells you" (John 2:5). And then, apparently, she simply walked away.

Can you see the situation and the setup? Jesus is left standing there with the servants looking to Him for a directive. His disciples are looking on as well. Mary had dropped the situation in His lap and left. Jesus was in a fix!

What had Mary done? She had set Him up and pushed Him far beyond His previous paradigm of ministry. How would He wiggle himself out of this situation?

We do not know how much time elapsed as Jesus stood there with the servants staring at Him, waiting for action. We do not know how long He struggled mentally and emotionally with what Mary had just done. If she had to do it, we can be sure He would have preferred for her to have done it in private rather than in the presence of the servants and His newly found disciples.

Jesus was in a fix!

John 2:6 tells us, "Now there were six stone water jars there for the Jewish rites of purification, each holding twenty or thirty gallons." These six water pots were for the wedding guests to wash their feet on their arrival and wash their hands before eating. The water was not for drinking, and the waiting servants must have been asking themselves, "What is He thinking? The people are waiting on us for wine, and He's doing nothing but looking at the water pots."

Imagine their utter shock when Jesus finally gave the directive, "Fill the water pots with water." Looking at one another, they must have wondered, *Is He kidding? Does He know how long it takes to fill these water pots?*

Filling those six water pots meant fetching a total of 120 to 180 gallons of water from the village well. (Remember, in those days, one did not simply turn on a faucet for water.) We do not know how far the well was from the house, how many trips the servants had to make, or how much grumbling took place as they were doing it, but we can well imagine how utterly surprised they were at the directive. In an act of obedience, however, they did what it took and filled the six water pots "up to the brim" (2:7).

"Okay," they must have thought to themselves, "Now that we have done all this work, let's see what He's going to do." But Jesus' next directive was just as confusing as the first. "And he said to them, 'Now draw some out and take it to the master of the feast'" (2:8).

How would you have handled that assignment? Would you have wondered if perhaps Jesus had drunk a little too much wine Himself? Probably, with much fear and anxiety, they took it to the master of the feast. He tasted it. They were probably awaiting his understandable surprise, and his shocked outburst. He did react—but in a different way than they all expected!

The scripture notes that after he had tasted the wine, the master of the feast called the bridegroom, and in the presence of the servants, said, "Everyone serves the good wine first, and when people have drunk freely, then the poor wine. But you have kept the good wine until now" (2:10). Something different, phenomenal, significant, and utterly supernatural had happened!

It wasn't supposed to happen that way. Jesus made it very clear to His mother that His time had not yet come. Mary heard Him very clearly, but then said to the servants, "Do whatever he tells you" (2:5). What did Mary do? She did what every good mother, every effective leader, does. She pushed Him into His hour. She pushed Him to acknowledge that His hour was present.[11]

> *She did what every good mother,*
> *every effective leader, does. She*
> *pushed Him into His hour.*

Many of us go through life thinking that our hour has not yet come. We back away from realities, opportunities, and options. We look at what our friends and neighbors are doing and decide that we should be doing the same. We are too afraid to pursue the things on our hearts for fear of being judged. Our friendships with, and commitment to, those who are stuck going nowhere force us to remain stuck with them. To put it metaphorically, we drive the same cars as them and feel compelled to park in the same spots.

One morning, I was rushing to catch a train from New York to Philadelphia and had just purchased a copy of a New York newspaper. My eyes and mind had captured the headline of the newly elected mayor of the great city of London in

England. To sum up the article, it spoke of Labour's representative Sadiq Khan, who had just been elected as London's first Muslim mayor. His life to date had been characterized by beating the odds, and he had just done it again.

One year earlier, as the Labour party looked toward the mayoral race, Mr. Khan was not a favorite, but he came in and won from behind—a recurring pattern to his career and his life. One of eight children born to working-class Pakistani immigrants, he showed from an early age a firm resolve to defy the odds, to turn his water into wine, to create success for himself and the causes important to him.

His wisdom, resolve, and capacity won for him the role of London's mayor—a job with a huge mandate and wide-ranging powers over one of the greatest cities in the world. He did not allow his race, his ethnicity, his religion, or the expectations of others to hold him back. He pushed forward day after day, month after month, year after year, until his dream was fulfilled.

Pursuing your dreams, however, will always draw criticism. I remember when I attended Bible college some of the leaders, I felt, did not like me. One day one of them appeared to confirm that assessment when he said to me, "Milton, your problem is that you insist on having a mind of your own."

That accusation has always baffled me. A mind of my own? What other mind would anyone expect me to have, given that God creates us as unique individuals? Having a mind of your own and surrounding yourself with others who are using and stretching their own minds is one of life's hidden secrets. People who actively use their God-given minds are like Mary—they can push us far beyond where we imagined we could go.

One of life's greatest tragedies is that we dream big dreams, then look around at other people's accomplishments (or lack thereof), and decide to remain parked and safe. We should thank God for those who kick us into a realization of our hour, our potential, our ability, our call, our gift, and our talents. The truth is, somebody always has to push us, since we very rarely move into life's new, challenging, changing experiences by ourselves. We all tend to back off when conflicts and crises arise, and believe that we just can't do it. We are not naturally programmed to see the seed that is in every need and the exciting opportunity in every challenge.

> *We all tend to back off when*
> *conflicts and crises arise, and*
> *believe that we just can't do it.*

Mary pushed Jesus into His hour, and He performed the miracle of turning water into wine. John 2:11 calls it the "beginning of miracles" (KJV). Not simply His *first* miracle, but the beginning of signs Jesus did. Your first significant risk of faith will be the beginning of your many miracles, life-changing events, and transformational experiences.

Jesus, the Son of God, was a great teacher, but He had never performed a miracle. He knew that His hour had come to call, teach, and train His disciples, but He did not recognize that it was also His hour to go into the deep, to launch out and to take the risk of faith into an area that He had never moved into.

We all experience this reality. We all stand at the brink and back off. We all come face to face with tremendous possibilities and close our eyes to them with a sense of being overwhelmed because we are unfamiliar with the place we now find ourselves in. When the individual who pushes or kicks us comes, how we respond determines our destiny. What will be your destiny?

Wisdom for Living

1. What is your understanding of Albert Einstein's statement, "There are only two ways to live your life; one is as though nothing is a miracle, the other is as though everything is a miracle"?

2. How do you think Jesus felt and what do you think He was saying to Himself when Mary confronted Him with the problem of the shortage of wine in the presence of the servants?

3. If you had been one of the servants who had to fill the pots with water, what would have said to the other servants as you took all those trips to the well to fill them?

4. When the master of the feast tasted the wine and summoned the bridegroom, what would you have expected him to say?

5. Who are some of the people who have pushed you into becoming who you are today?

Chapter 6

My Passion: To Learn, Grow, and Serve

There is something powerful in having a clear and early sense of one's call. I grew up with it and remained conscious of it. I always knew it, and I was blessed to be a part of a church with a youth group that was active in ministry. Many of us were out doing street meetings, home Bible studies, and revival meetings. Pastor Smith would drive us to different parts of the country to conduct revivals and youth meetings. On many Friday nights, we held street meetings, winning people to the Lord, and on Sundays at 6 p.m., it was our custom to attend youth fellowship, followed by the evening service.

Life-Changing Messages on Tithing

When my pastor began teaching a series of messages on tithing, I remember being aware that he had not taught on the topic before. My only recollection of tithing was of singing the refrain of the song, "Hear the Pennies Dropping" (Fidellia H. Dewitt),[12] which went like this:

> Dropping, dropping, dropping, dropping
> Hear those pennies fall.
>
> Every one for Jesus,
> We would give them all.

That was indeed a powerful song for us at that age, and believe it or not, pennies were all that we had. But now, as we were growing up and many of us had part-time jobs, our concept of stewardship had to be upgraded. Our pastor began to challenge us to give God our lives, our time, our talents and our abilities—and to see everything we have and who we are as gifts from God.

Our pastor began to challenge us to give God our lives, our time, our talents and our abilities.

A tithe is a one-tenth portion of one's income given back to God as a contribution to God's work. The tithe is a "first fruit" of your increase. The principle behind a tithe as our first fruit is the fact that God is our source of supply. He is the cause and source of our blessings and prosperity. Therefore, the tithe is not any tenth of one's income; it is the first tenth of one's income.

Leviticus 23:10 states, "Speak to the people of Israel and say to them, When you come into the land that I give you and reap its harvest, you shall bring the sheaf of the first fruits of your harvest to the priest." I remember listening to my pastor and saying to myself, "I have no money, and I cannot tithe what I don't have." As the series of messages continued, an idea grabbed my mind.

Several days later, when I saw him alone in the back of our church, I decided to take advantage of this private moment to share my idea. I said to him, "Brother Smith, I don't have any money to tithe. I don't get any allowance, but I have an idea. I go to school Mondays to Fridays, and I am free on Saturdays. I could come to your house on Saturday mornings and do whatever you want done. This will be my tithe. I'll bathe the dog, wash your car, dig the weeds out of the flower bed, and do whatever you and Sister Smith want me to do. I will do it every Saturday as my tithe." He stood there and looked intently at me as I was sharing. Then he remarked, "I will get back to you on that." A week later, he indicated that he would take me up on my offer.

Every Saturday morning thereafter I walked about six or seven miles to my pastor's house to "pay" my tithe. I bathed the dog, washed the car, dug out the weeds, and boxed Sunday school materials for the outlying churches in the country. I did whatever they needed me to do.

At about 12:30 in the afternoon, Sister Smith would call me upstairs to wash up, and she would give me a sandwich, a boiled egg, and a glass of milk. This was a new experience for me because up to that time, I had only received a glass of milk once a year at Christmas and a whole egg once a year for my birthday. Lunch on Saturdays was a treat that I thoroughly enjoyed.

After lunch, I would sit in Pastor Smith's library and read some of his books before walking back another six or seven miles to the home where I was staying. Being in his study and reading his books both excited and fascinated me. It opened my mind, enlarged my appetite for books, and set me on a journey of searching for knowledge that I remain on to this day.

> *Being in his study and reading his books both excited and fascinated me.*

One day, some high school friends and I were discussing some community ministry ideas I had developed to touch the lives of the students in our school—Saturday seminars to help neighborhood children with their schoolwork as well as sports activities and other programs as ways of relating to and connecting with teenagers. The group was very excited about the ideas. They all wanted to be part of it.

There was just one problem: while I had made the proposal, I told my friends I would not be able to participate on Saturdays. One of them asked me, "What is it that you do every Saturday morning?" I explained that I went to my pastor's house and performed whatever tasks he assigned to me as my tithe to God.

His reaction and response both shocked and hurt me. He turned to the group and said, "Milton can't come on Saturdays. He has decided to become the pastor's slave." I remember hearing people say that sticks and stones could break your bones, but words could never harm you. That day, I discovered that the saying was not true. It was as if my friend had punched me in the stomach—a hard knockout punch!

My friends began to laugh, and I knew that in the next few days that statement, "Milton is the pastor's slave," would be circulated throughout the school. I felt the pain and embarrassment of his statement every time I heard the laughter it created in my high school. And yet, I encouraged myself with the fact that, in spite of the pain, I had made the right and wise decision.

I remember one day after completing my routine chores, Sister Smith called me upstairs to wash up, and we sat around the kitchen table talking. Pastor Smith joined us. We were having a wonderful time when she made a statement that shocked me: "Milton, Brother Smith and I can't wait to attend your graduation from college."

I choked and then asked, "What did you say?"

She repeated, "Brother Smith and I can't wait to attend your graduation from college."

Up to that point, no one—absolutely no one—had ever mentioned college to me before. I had never seen myself as college material. Later on that day, as I walked the many miles to where I was staying, I continued to think about what she said, staggering at the thought.

I had never seen myself as college material.

Over the next several months, the pastor and his wife both noticed my doubts and continued to reinforce the idea of college. After a while, I came to realize that they honestly believed it. They saw something in me and believed something about me that I had not perceived at that time.

From that day on, whenever I was finished serving them, I would spend much of my time in my pastor's study, reading and becoming exposed to great theological writers. Sister Smith had planted something in me—an idea, a dream, a desire to learn, study and see things with new eyes—seeds in my spirit that continue to live and grow there to this day.

If I was going to prepare for college, my next big challenge was to find someone to help me upgrade my academics—someone who would be willing to tutor me at no cost. I decided to ask Joy Bradford, one of several young ladies in our church whom I considered quite brilliant. Joy lived with her grandmother, and I thought that, along with asking her if she would be willing to tutor me, I should also ask her to check if her grandmother was comfortable with my coming to her home two afternoons a week. Fortunately, her grandmother agreed to the plan.

Many afternoons as I was being tutored, I saw Joy's grandmother peeping through a slight opening of her bedroom door, watching the process. I sensed that she was happy with Joy's tutoring work—and so was I! Two afternoons a week after school, I visited Joy's home for help with subjects like mathematics, geography, geometry, and the like. As the tutoring process continued and as I was becoming more comfortable with my progress, it was becoming more clear to me purpose and passion are linked together to help one make the painful decisions that creative living requires.

As Aristotle said, "It is impossible even to think without a mental picture." My new thoughts and emerging mental pictures of my long-term purpose became like movies playing inside of my mind. These "mental movies" caused me to commit myself to acquiring whatever I was lacking, whatever would block me from reaching and fulfilling what I believed was God's purpose for my life.

This was the beginning of a new, mind-stretching process for me. Even though I could not have adequately verbalized it at that time, I can more clearly see the process that I was pursuing. It was a process of creating new mental pictures of my future, effective self. Joy, thank you very much for the significant investment you made in me.

> ### *This was the beginning of a new,*
> ### *mind-stretching process for me.*

Looking back after all these years, I can agree with Dr. Seuss's statement in his wonderful book *I Can Read with My Eyes Shut* [13] : "The more that you read, the more things you will know. The more that you learn, the more places you'll go." Today that reflects my story.

These experiences helped me to understand the blessings and benefits of trusting God and being faithful to Him through tithes and offerings. I realized that the 10 percent of what one earns is not all that belongs to God—everything one has belongs to God. Ten percent is not a big requirement in the light of the abundant mercies God daily gives to you and me.

Imagine then, how happy and excited I was decades later, when I proposed to a young lady named Hyacinth who is now my wife, to discover that from childhood she had been taught the principle and practice of tithing by her father, the Rev. Douglas C. J. Bobb.

Over the decades, my wife and I have had the privilege of tithing to the Lord and seeing Him fulfill His Malachi 3:10–13 promise.

> Bring the full tithe into the storehouse, that there may be food in my house. And thereby put me to the test, says the LORD of hosts, if I will not open the windows of heaven for you and pour down for you a blessing until there is no more need. I will rebuke the devourer for you, so that it will not destroy the fruits of your soil, and your vine in the field shall not fail to bear, says the LORD of hosts. Then all nations will call you blessed, for you will be a land of delight, says the LORD of hosts.

Become a person of financial integrity. Give God the portion of your time, talents, abilities and resources that He requires, and watch Him open doors for you and grant you blessings that are "pressed down, shaken together, running over" (Luke 6:38).

I honestly believe that God is looking for people through whom He can do big things, even the impossible.

Unfortunately, so many people feel more comfortable doing just the things they can do by themselves. Partner with God now and do the impossible! *Do it now*!

Wisdom for Living

1. What can you remember about how I developed my passion for teaching?
2. How did I develop my passion for leading?
3. How did I develop my passion for giving?
4. What do you see as the benefits of sharing the Bible knowledge you have with others?
5. What do you see as the benefits of becoming actively involved in the ministries of the church?
6. What do you see as the benefits of sharing whatever you have so that you can contribute to God's glory?

Chapter 7

Life Offers Horses to Those Who Would Ride

Count your blessings, not your problems. We must be willing to let go of the life we have planned, so as to accept the life that God has waiting for us.

—Joseph Campbell, 1904–1987

Safe horse riding involves a delicate balance of necessary effort and skill. Jockeys who hope to win must stay focused, fit, and strong. They must see opportunities, make decisions under pressure, and be open to accept guidance from experienced trainers.

Every owner of race horses keeps his or her eyes open to find and develop a great rider. Great riders bring physical preparation and the mental toughness that the sport requires.

The skills necessary for success in the sport of horse racing are also necessary for success in all of life. Mental toughness could be described as the psychological edge that enables you to cope with the many demands and pressures of life and remain more determined, focused, controlled, and consistent than others. People who gain this edge realize that it comes from the discipline to see and effectively use the gifts, talents, and opportunities God has given them. They think and live differently. They are both positive and resilient. They have learned how to face whatever is thrown at them and cooperate with God to achieve a result that is consistent with His will for their lives. These people are the riders to whom life offers horses.

Here is another of life's secrets: Never seek permission from anyone to be yourself, but do not confuse permission with counsel, guidance, and wisdom from others.

I traveled from Guyana formerly known as "British Guiana" to Trinadad and entered the West Indies Bible Institute in in May 1960 to study for the Christian ministry. During those four years I, like all the other students, studied in the mornings and worked in the woodshop each afternoon. In the woodshop we made different types of furniture that was then sold to help support the institution. Along with this, several students were selected to pastor different congregations on the weekends, and I was one of them. I finally graduated in 1964. I had worked very hard to raise the needed money to invite my mother to travel to Trinidad to attend my graduation.

Never seek permission from anyone to be yourself, but do not confuse permission with counsel, guidance, and wisdom from others.

Oliver Warner, a friend of our family who lived in Trinidad, was sitting next to my mother. Watching the tears flow from my mother's eyes during the graduation exercise, she turned to my mother and remarked, "Miss Edna, those must be tears of joy." Wiping her eyes, my mother replied, "No dear, they are tears of regret and shame. I really really gave him hell."

It was indeed hell at the time, but much later those hard times enabled me to experience the dependability, faithfulness of God, and dimensions of heaven on earth. The realm of faith never has a dress rehearsal; there is no practice, absolutely none. It's like learning to swim. You can't learn how to swim while lying on the beach. The person who is afraid to get into the water, who looks at the water and says, "My time has not yet come," will never learn to swim and will never be able to jump in and save a person who is drowning.

If I had listened to those who discouraged me from participating in my church and committing not only my heart but my entire life to God, to those who discouraged me from doing chores for my pastor as my tithe, or to any of those other voices of rejection, I would never have graduated from college and gone on to fulfill my purpose as a pastor, teacher, and leader.

The Need May Be Your Hour

At the wedding at Cana, Jesus, the Son of God was convinced that His time had not yet come. He heard no special call, saw no angel visitation or opening skies, heard no thunder, and saw no flash of lightning. There was no prophetic voice from heaven thundering, "THIS IS YOUR HOUR." This all changed when there was a need. When confronted by the need, His mother pushed Him into His hour so that the need could be met. When pushed, Jesus discovered that His hour was always there. His gifts and abilities were always there. His anointing was always there. His hour was always there, but He never knew it until His mother pushed Him.

All of us, if we will indeed grow, need those individuals who are courageous enough to push us. The greatest problem is that few of us really understand when we are being pushed. Those who really care about us may push us, but our enemies also push us for different reasons. They push us hoping to destroy us, to harm us, to prevent us from fulfilling our dreams and purposes.

All of us, if we will indeed grow, need those individuals who are courageous enough to push us.

Only when we are pushed do we get into the waters and discover that God is able, that we can actually swim and survive. "Even though I walk through the valley of the shadow of death, I will fear no evil, for you are with me; your rod and your staff, they comfort me" (Psalm 23:4). Only when we are pushed do we discover that underneath are His everlasting arms (Deut. 33:27).

In response to the need and to being pushed forward by His mother, Jesus performed a miracle "and manifested His glory. And His disciples believed on Him" (John 2:11). It's interesting that only then did His disciples—those who were following Him, listening to Him, and being taught and trained by Him—believe in Him.

People believe in us when they see us survive the risks of faith. They don't believe in us because we're good preachers or teachers or nice individuals or good persons. They believe in us when they see us take and survive risks, go through the valleys, and plunge into deep waters believing God—and then they see God come through on our behalf. Churches grow because people believe, and people believe when they see us survive the risks of faith.

What are you hearing? It is more important that you understand a message rather than enjoy it. You can enjoy a message that you don't understand, yet you cannot grow through things that you don't understand. This is why it is important to understand. Jesus spoke in parables so that people might understand. He gave them pictures and kept it very simple so that they might understand.

We have to be pushed to act on something even if we don't like to be pushed, which is more often than not. Eventually, after we succeed we are always glad for the person(s) who caused us to take the risk.

To grow you must take risks. There will always be people who will criticize you, and those who will follow you yet still criticize you, *but* there will also always be people who will believe in you. Some of those people may push you, others may not; in fact, it is often true that our enemies push us more than our friends. When we refuse to take risks, when we choose to stay in safe, familiar, unthreatening places and situations, we get stuck until the right people come and push us along the continuum of our purpose.

Mary did not say, "You can do it." She set up a scenario where Jesus was left standing where the servants were looking, and guess who else was looking: His disciples. The guests did not know there was no wine, but His disciples were looking at Him, so on one side the servants were saying, "Do something" while on the other side the disciples were saying, "What can He do?"

Mary's push is what paved the way for Jesus to develop a ministry of miracles. He had never done it before, but from that point on, He did it. He opened the eyes of the blind, made the crooked straight, raised the dead, and cleansed the leper—all because Mary pushed Him to do something when, as He said, "My time has not yet come." Jesus' eyes became opened to the many possibilities of His mission.

Mary's push is what paved the way for Jesus to develop a ministry of miracles.

Needs Are Addressed through Projects, and Projects Require Leadership

The story of Jesus turning water into wine illustrates at least three leadership principles. First, meaningful projects emerge when pressing needs are discovered. The shortage of wine produced a need that became Jesus's project. Second, all success in life and all miracles you can create depend on how well you handle individual projects. As previously discussed, after being pushed, Jesus' response and how He handled the situation paved the way for Him to perform many more miracles thereafter. Third, each project requires the appropriate tools, but the tools alone are not enough and can accomplish very little if project leadership is not in place. In the case of the wedding in Cana, there were many people present at the wedding: the bride, the groom, their parents, their friends and loved ones, additional family members, the servants, Jesus, Mary, and the disciples who Jesus had invited, but there was not a clearly identified leader.

This illustrates the importance of the need for leadership in resolving the needs of people. All of the individuals at the wedding in Cana had different skill sets and might have had a shared interest in the outcome. However, they had no experience in working with each other and no clear single vision of the solution to the problem, and so it would have been impossible for them to suddenly become a functioning unit capable of navigating all of the issues involved in solving this problem. When Mary was informed of the need, she understood it, assessed it, and realized that Jesus was the only one present who could provide the leadership needed to remedy the situation. She also understood that every reluctant leader must be pushed into his or her destiny, and therefore she pushed Jesus into His.

As leaders, we need to understand that every project requires a leader. Leadership is so important in that a leader without the team can still accomplish more and be more effective than a team without a leader. An effective leader understands that every need or project involves dealing with an environment that one must safely navigate in order to avoid pitfalls and landmines that could sabotage the expected outcome.

> *As leaders, we need to understand that every project requires a leader.*

All leaders and most people grow when they are pushed, whether by circumstances or other people. We determine whether our response will be negative or positive, a response that pushes us forward in growth or a response that pushes us backward and downward. Your response may not always impact other people, but it will always impact you.

We sometimes miss the fact that God may very well be stirring the waters. Take a moment now and look back at your life. Focus on the faithfulness of God to you—in spite of you—and realize that it was God stirring up the waters, irritating your spirit, creating a change, moving people to push you when all the while you were blaming and rebuking Satan. Satan hates faith. He knows the awesome power of faith. Move forward in faith to change your water into wine. Do it now!

Wisdom for Living

1. What is your understanding of the phrase "Life offers horses to those who would ride"? What do you think my mother was experiencing as she was sitting through my graduation ceremony?

2. What do you think she meant when she said to her friend, "No dear, they're not tears of joy. They are tears of regret and shame. I actually gave him hell"?

3. What do you think enables some individuals to use their hellish experiences and cooperate with God to create heaven?

4. Why does every project require the appropriate leadership?

Chapter 8

The Power of Purpose
and integrity

In 1967, I visited with Brother Alkins of the Christian Mission Church at his stall in the Bourda market in Georgetown, Guyana. The main products in his store were children and women's colorful underwear. He knew me while I was active as a leader in the National Youth for Christ movement and City wide youth evangelism. He also remembered that I had left several years earlier to attend Bible College in Trinadad and that I had since returned and was now pastoring two congregations of the Church of God in the city of Georgetown.

I informed him that I had made the decision to travel to the United States to get married to my fiancée, Hyacinth, daughter of the Rev. D. C. J. Bobb, whom he knew, and also to continue my studies and ministry. As I had no money, I asked him for a major favor, which was to consider trusting me as a Christian brother and advancing to me a large inventory of underwear to sell house to house. I assured him that I would collect the inventory each day, travel outside of the city, sell them house to house, and return with his money before the market closed.

He questioned me to make sure he heard me clearly. He then called his wife to hear what I was suggesting, and they both agreed to give me the inventory to sell on a daily basis. That very day they allowed me to take several dozen pieces of underwear in a large cardboard box. I placed the box on the handle of my bicycle and rode several miles outside the city. I sold every single one and returned with his money half an hour before the market closed, just as I had promised.

Each day I did the same for several weeks and by so doing, was able to raise the amount of money needed to travel from Guyana in South America to Philadelphia in United States to fulfill my purpose. The life lesson I learned from that experience is this: God positions people to help you if you and they are clear about your integrity, passion, and purpose.

God positions people to help you if you and they are clear about your integrity, passion, and purpose.

Wisdom for Living

1. How does having a sense of purpose and integrity open one's eyes to see risk taking possibilities that few individuals see or consider?
2. What do you think went through Brother Alkins' mind when I, a pastor of two churches in the city, made to him the proposal of marketing those products?
3. What are some of the ways through which integrity connected to one's practice can help to lead one to success in life?

Chapter 9

Transition from Guyana South America to Philadelphia

Hyacinth Bobb and I were engaged in Guyana. Her father, the Rev. D. C. J. Bobb, had been an outstanding pastor of the Bedford Methodist Church in the city of Georgetown, as well as a highly recognized leader in Guyana. There he served in a number of national positions as well as the chairman of the National Ecumenical Council. Before the country gained its independence from England, Rev. Bobb had been appointed by the British governor to serve on a special National Commission of Advisors during a season of political unrest.

He had traveled to the United States to participate in a special program of Marriage and Family Therapy led by Drs. David and Margaret Meade. He and his wife were also active in the field of education and started what became a prominent high school in Guyana.

Earlier, in 1965, President Lyndon B. Johnson of the United States of America initiated the Model Cities Program as part of his War on Poverty. It led to the development of more than 150 program experiments to develop new antipoverty initiatives and alternative forms of municipal government. These programs were designed to enable churches, schools, and community to work together for the betterment of all involved.

Due to Rev. Bobb's proven expertise and significant contribution at a national level in Guyana, and based on a recommendation by Drs. David and Margaret Meade, the United Methodist Church in Philadelphia asked him to relocate to Philadelphia with his family so that he might be instrumental as part of a team in helping the church become more effective and share in the development of the Model City's program and other initiatives.

This resulted in the migration of his family to the United States. However, since his eldest child Hyacinth was born in Saint Vincent while he was pastoring there, she had to remain in Guyana while her travel documents were being processed.

In 1964 I had graduated from the West Indies Bible Institute in Trinidad. In 1962, during my second year of theological training, I became a "student pastor" of the Marabella Church of God in the Marabella area of Trinidad. After graduation, I continued to enjoy a fantastic fellowship and relationship with people of that congregation, and we experienced much growth.

The leadership of the Church of God in Guyana wrote to me about returning to Guyana and accepting the pastorate of both the John Street and the Bel Air Street congregations in the city of Georgetown. Frankly, with all the political unrest in the country at that time, I was not interested.

Several months later, however, I experienced a type of divine visitation in which I sensed God saying to me, "If you obey Me and leave the pastorate you enjoy so much in Trinadad and return to Guyana, I will show you the wife I have chosen for you there." Wow! I certainly became interested. Still, leaving that congregation was a very painful experience. A good number of young people had been won to the Lord, yet I knew I had to leave. I accepted Guyana's invitation and in a short while returned to serve there.

> *"If you obey Me and leave the pastorate you enjoy so much in Trinadad and return to Guyana, I will show you the wife I have chosen for you there."*

Imagine my disappointment on my arrival to discover that no one had made any provision for my housing. Trevor Isaacs, a member of the Bel Air Street congregation, suggested that his aunt, a teacher who lived alone, might be willing to let me share a room in her home if I took care of my meals. This arrangement worked out very well.

Trevor's aunt noticed, however, that I was quite helpless in the kitchen. She suggested I make arrangements to have my main meals with her sister's family, the Hazelwoods.

After a season of deep consultation between her and the Hazelwoods, Trevor's aunt said to me, " We have a niece who would make you an excellent minister's wife. She's the daughter of the prominent Methodist minister, the Rev. Dr. C.J. Bobb." She found out that my birthday was coming up soon, and said, "I will plan a small birthday party and invite her so that you can meet her." I was both interested and intrigued.

At the party, Trevor's aunt enthusiastically introduced me to Miss Hyacinth Bobb. Her parents and siblings had already left Guyana for Philadelphia in the United States, and she planned to follow them as soon as her papers were processed.

There was an instant attraction on both sides. Could she be the person the Lord had spoken to me about when I was in Trinadad? Everyone who knew her spoke very highly of her. In our conversations together we connected very easily. We both had a passion for God and the desire to serve him all of our lives. We continued to see one another, and we both became more and more comfortable in each other's company.

One day I shared with her what I sensed the Lord had spoken to me in Trinidad—that on my return to Guyana, he would show me the wife he had chosen for me. Without hesitation she said, "Well, the Lord and I have a good relationship, and he hasn't said a thing to me. He had better start talking!" She asked that we not see each other for two weeks while we sought the Lord's will. We both went into serious prayer and fasting, seeking clarity about God's will for our lives and if we were indeed the ones He had chosen for each other.

> *We both went into serious prayer*
> *and fasting, seeking clarity about*
> *God's will for our lives*

After a few days she returned to say that she felt the Lord was indeed giving her peace about me being the man for her to marry. Being satisfied in my spirit, being a man of action, and knowing that she would soon leave the country to join her family in Philadelphia, I proposed—just one month after we met! Since her parents were out of the country, she said I would have to write to her father, seeking permission to have her hand in marriage. And so I did.

Immediately, frantic phone calls began to be made back and forth to family and friends. Who could this young man be? What does anyone know about his background, his family, and his ability to support a family? After much investigation, her father gave his blessing, and when she finally left Guyana to join her family in Philadelphia, we were engaged. That led to my own transition to Philadelphia in May of 1967—to reconnect with Hyacinth, to be married, and to pursue graduate studies. Immediately upon arriving in Philadelphia, I connected myself with the High Street Church of God in the Germantown section of the city.

Chapter 10

My Night in a Smelly Philadelphia Prison Cell

After relocating from Guyana to Philadelphia to be reunited with my fiancée, I settled into a weekly pattern of church attendance. Each Sunday morning and Wednesday night I traveled by bus from North Philadelphia to the Germantown area of the city to attend services at the High Street Church of God.

One Wednesday evening in the summer of 1967, I was traveling by the number 23 trolley on my way to a midweek service. Suddenly, I experienced my first-ever nosebleed! I grabbed my handkerchief, covered my nose, got off the bus at the next stop, and stood on the street, trying to deal with the nosebleed. I was wearing a dark pair of dress pants and a long-sleeved white shirt, my New Testament in my shirt pocket.

A police car approached where I was standing, and I immediately looked around to see why they were stopping, but nothing else was going on. An officer approached me and took my name and address. "Where are you going?" he asked.

"I'm going to a midweek prayer meeting at the High Street Church of God in Germantown," I responded, still holding my handkerchief to my nose.

"You're going to church, eh?" Grabbing me, he said, "You fit the description of the man who just tried to rob the bar two blocks away, and you're coming with me."

I was immediately handcuffed by the officer and pushed into the police car. The officer's name was Knorr. No amount of explanation availed. I was taken to the 39th Police District precinct of the city, booked, and placed in a cell to await a court hearing the next morning.

> *I was immediately handcuffed by the*
> *officer and pushed into the police car.*

"Can I make a phone call to my fiancée or her father to let them know where I am?" I asked. His response was a quick bark: "We don't make phone calls here."

My misery was compounded when I was placed in this very small cell with a man who was drunk and had vomited and urinated on the floor. There was no bed. He was sitting on the floor, and I had to find a spot on the floor saturated by his urine and vomit.

About 9:45 the next morning, I was taken into a room to stand before the judge. It was a relatively short proceeding.

After my name was called and I approached the bench, I was asked to state my full name and address. Then the judge carefully looked at me, shuffled some papers on his desk, and finally uttered one sentence: "Go home and learn to behave yourself." I was released.

I was relieved to be free, yet dumfounded, shocked, and thunderstruck. For a moment, I wondered if I had just awakened from a nightmare. I left the precinct very upset, angry, confused, and lost. Angry and upset because it all seemed so unbelievable; confused and lost because, having left the precinct and being new to the city, I had difficulty finding my way back home and being able to fully explain what I had just experienced. What an introduction to the Philadelphia criminal justice system!

I was relieved to be free, yet dumbfounded, shocked, and thunderstruck.

Every Setback Is a Potential Setup

The evening in jail and my brief morning appearance before the judge had infiltrated my psyche and impacted me emotionally and psychologically. The judge's words kept replaying in my mind: "Go home and learn to behave yourself"—what absurd legal abuse! How would it shape my life? How was I supposed to respond? Even now, decades later, I still find it hard to fully capture the true depth of my emotions and the impact this experience made on my life.

Over the next several days and months I began reflecting on the emotional impact of having to spend that night sitting on the dirty, smelly, urine- and vomit-saturated floor of that prison cell. I began to retrace my life's journey to that point.

I thought of the Sunday night beatings I had received as a teenager because of my faith and my interest in serving God.

I relived the pain and embarrassment of being beaten by my brother in the churchyard on a Sunday evening, before the eyes of other youth group members.

I recalled the constant threats from my family, followed by the emotional trauma of that Sunday morning when all my belongings were thrown out of the house and I was made homelessness and abandoned at age fourteen.

My mind went back to each day I faced my friends at high school who called me "the white man's slave" because of my commitment to spend my Saturday mornings at my pastor's home, serving him and his wife as my tithe to God.

We all experience similar "bitter waters" continually, and we see our Lord perform the daily miracle of changing them to fine wine. We can go through life reflecting and thinking of all the pain, the challenges, the disappointments, the let-downs and the trauma of our journey, or we can believe that turning bitter water into wine is possible, and trust God for the miracles.

We all experience similar "bitter waters" continually, and we see our Lord perform the daily miracle of changing them to fine wine.

I decided to positively embrace all of my experiences and to commit myself to make every effort, to work hard, study hard, and allow every bitter experience to contribute to my spiritual growth and the building of God's kingdom.

Every Donut Has a Hole

Who walks into a donut shop and complains about the holes? No, we buy donuts, knowing that every donut has a hole. The same is true with every experience in life. To focus all our attention on the challenging and painful holes that come our way is to rob ourselves of the personal strength and power of the total experience. Over the decades, my wife and I have sought to stay focused on the donuts, lest we get distracted and overwhelmed by the holes.

The winds of life are always blowing, and are liable to blow you off course, but if you stay focused on God, He will guide you to your purposed destination. Joseph, in Genesis 41:51–52, gave names to his two sons to sum up the benefits he reaped by remaining anchored in his faith of God. It says, "Joseph called the name of the firstborn Manasseh [*to forget*]. 'For,' he said, 'God has made me forget all my hardship and all my father's house.' The name of the second he called Ephraim [*fruitful*], 'For God has made me fruitful in the land of my affliction.'"

Wisdom for Living

1. How would you have handled this night of imprisonment?

2. How do you think Jesus would have handled this painful experience?

3. Read in Genesis 41:51–52 how Joseph handled his years of struggle after being sold by his brothers to become a slave in Egypt. Does this passage reflect his reaction or his response, and what insights can you gain from it?

Chapter 11

A Tribute to My Wife, the Rev. Dr. Hyacinth Bobb Grannum

I n my preface to this book, I took the opportunity to express my profound gratitude to my dear and loving wife, the Rev. Dr. Hyacinth Bobb Grannum, who has encouraged and supported me for over fifty years as of this writing. She has been and continues to be a significant blessing, a precious gift from God to me.

"An excellent wife who can find? She is far more precious than jewels" (Proverbs 31:10). Well, the truth is, I did not actually find her. Many persons who knew her well, found her for me. In introducing her to me, they painted a picture of her that was clear, fascinating, captivating, intriguing, and attractive. They were convinced that we were well suited for each other, and time has indeed proven how right they were.

She is a God-fearing, committed Christian, the eldest daughter of an outstanding nationally known Methodist pastor who was a government leader. Both he and his wife were also educators.

Sometimes, a good person is not always the right person. But after we had spent much time in prayer, God showed us both that we were right for each other.

I remain extremely thankful to God for the ability He has given me to listen, observe, analyze, and to finally respect the wisdom of the people He has put into my life over the years and who have offered me important insights, discernment, and guidance.

In assessing our friendship and now over fifty years of marriage to this point, my dear wife is indeed a hard worker, a positive influence and an excellent example of the Proverbs 31 woman in the Bible.

She continues to bless me with her total self. She has a godly character, a deep and proven faith in God, profound caring for me, our children, our grandchildren and our larger and extended families as well as for others. She is blessed with a spirit of diligence and passionate intercession. She inspires others to noble living, creative leadership, humble service, compassionate caring, and authentic faith.

She continues to bless me with her total self.

As a wife, a mother, co-founder and co-pastor of the New Covenant Church of Philadelphia, its local, national and international ministries, her people skills and leadership ability are indeed proven. She is blessed with integrity and discipline. She maintains a daily life of service, taking care of herself and her family, praying with and for people, counseling others, making phone calls, writing letters, sending text messages, and the like.

With much sensitivity, she guides my actions and reactions with the gentle wisdom and persuasion of an intuitive wife.

Everybody needs somebody and wants to be needed by somebody. Everybody wants to be something, and we all appreciate those who help us succeed. Jesus needed Mary, who pushed him into doing something and becoming something earlier than He planned. My wife has helped me become, and continues to help me become, the person God designed me to be.

I cannot say thanks enough for the quality of her investment in me over the years—her faithful, loving support, thoughtfulness, prayerful undergirding, cheerful encouragement, and partnership during our decades of marriage, child-rearing, and demanding ministry.

My words cannot fully express the gratitude which overflows in my spirit for the many years she encouraged, supported, and sacrificed while I pursued leadership development and graduate studies.

Our Wedding—and a Thirteen-Hour Bus Trip
to Our Honeymoon

I arrived in the United States in May 1965, in time for the graduation of my fiancée. Both she and her mother, Mrs. Myrtle Bobb, were among the first graduates of the newly opened Community College of Philadelphia. It was a much acclaimed and historic event.

Since she and I had been apart for over two years, corresponding only by weekly letters, I suggested that we get married as soon as possible. "Married! That's not in our family plans," Hyacinth exclaimed. Her words were echoed by her father when he heard the request, but after a couple of weeks, her parents decided they would arrange for us to get married.

Saturday, September 2nd, during the Labor Day weekend, was the date planned. There was great excitement as the news spread quickly through the three churches of the Midtown Parish of the Philadelphia Methodist Church.

Memorial Temple was the church pastored by her father, the Rev. Dr. C.J. Bobb. The Seventh Street Methodist Church and the St. John's Methodist Church, along with Hyacinth's father, the Rev. J. Nye, the Rev. Frank Kensil, and Bishop Frederick Talbot, of the AME Church, all participated in the ceremony.

For our wedding, the Lord blessed us in many ways. Hyacinth's college friends give her a bridal shower, while the ladies of the three churches in the parish got together and gave her a second bridal shower.

"Married! That's not in our family plans," Hyacinth exclaimed.

I was responsible for the honeymoon, of course. My aunt, nurse Ruby Grannum King, helped me arrange with a cousin of ours, the Rev. Arnold Bruce, to use his home in Tennessee for a week while he and his family were on vacation. So at midnight, after the wedding, we left by bus for the thirteen-hour trip to Greenville, Tennessee.

Our hosts had informed their neighbors about our arrival, and they gave us a very warm welcome. Mrs. Bruce had prepared a full, delicious dinner for us, with much variety, and made us feel very much cared for. Two highlights of our honeymoon are worth mentioning. We saw an advertisement for a movie that we decided to see. Our next-door neighbors called a taxi for us, and told us what the appropriate fare plus tip should be. Mind you, neither Hyacinth nor I was a movie-goer, so we missed some clues when we chose to see *The Graduate*!

After the movie (a shock in itself), we decided to walk back "home," because we didn't think it was very far. (We were pretty sure the taxi driver had taken advantage of us since we were visitors, and had taken a far longer route than necessary.) We remembered being on the main highway quite a while, so we got there and proceeded to walk, looking for signs or markers to help us get back.

Not long afterwards, a police car pulled up alongside of us and stopped to question us. We explained that we were strangers, from Philadelphia, with no money and on our honeymoon. "Get into this car," the officer replied. His words seemed rough, but something in his tone made us, especially Hyacinth, feel safe. You can imagine the looks of the neighbors' faces when they saw us returning to the house in a police car!

Another day, Hyacinth suggested a picnic in a meadow we had seen one day on our walk. So we left at midmorning, intending to spend pretty much all day there. We had just finished a delicious brunch when we spotted some cows at one corner of the meadow. All of a sudden, Hyacinth recalled the stories she had heard about cows and red garments. (She was wearing a bright red skirt.)

> *You can imagine the looks of the neighbors' faces when they saw us returning to the house in a police car!*

We both turned to look at the cows only to realize, to our dismay, that one was most definitely charging ahead in our direction. Where our energy and speed came from, I don't know, but in record time we gathered our things, threw them in our picnic basket, and scrambled out of there. We had settled near a small stream, with a bridge nearby. Since we had no time to make it to the bridge, I leaped over the stream, leaving Hyacinth to gather her skirt and copy my action.

Later, in recounting the experience, she said that she learned from the time of our honeymoon not to lean on me but on God, as she had done all of her life.

Over the years, many have been the streams we have had to jump over. But with God's help and because of our obedience to Him and commitment to our family and ministry, He has made us fruitful in our many undertakings. My dear wife has helped me to develop new eyes to see things differently, to catch new meanings in experiences, and to turn many of our waters into wine.

With her by my side, I have been able to turn fall and winter into spring and summer. Like the American poet Robert Loveman, she has helped me to see beyond the normal. Loveman saw and experienced the heavy rainfall, yet he focused not on the rain but the good it produces. Hyacinth and Loveman have helped me to both see and sing:

> It isn't raining rain to me,
> It's raining daffodils;
> In every dimpled drop I see
> Wild flowers on the hills.[14]

Wisdom For Living

1. Why is earnest prayer really necessary in making the big decision about this selecting of a spouse?
2. If couples really believe that God put them together, why is it important to maintain that consciousness through the different seasons of marriage?
3. What is the role of gratitude and respect for each other in the building and maintaining of a healthy marriage?
4. What are some of the evidences of respect for each other?

Chapter 12

How God Delivered Me from the Murderous Plans of Idi Amin

A cts 12 states that King Herod Agrippa killed the apostle James, the brother of John. It is wise to study how the early Christians dealt with trying circumstances and how they handled their hours of danger and distress. At this time, the Christian church was in a state of great suffering. King Herod's killing of James pleased the people and motivated him to capture and imprison Peter, condemning him to a similar terrible execution.

Herod Agrippa (10 BC–44 AD) was a Judean monarch and the grandson of Herod the Great during the first century AD. He is the king named Herod in the Acts of the Apostles in the Bible and was also known in his time as "Agrippa the Great."[15]

As king of Rome, Agrippa ruled over a territory as great as that of his grandfather. Unlike Herod the Great, however, Agrippa seems to have been highly popular among the Jews. Although extravagant in his youth, he was careful to observe Jewish customs as king and was able to perform several services for which he is recognized by Jewish sources with gratitude.

To the Christians, however, Agrippa became an enemy because of his repression of the new leaders of the Christian faith. Accounts of his death, at games held in Caesarea in 44 AD, differ. Josephus, an eminent Jewish scholar,[16] and Acts agree that he died after being declared as speaking with the voice of a deity. However, Acts implies divine retribution, while Josephus sees the death as an act of fate. Other Jewish traditions hold the Romans responsible for his death, due to their jealousy of Agrippa's popularity and fear of a possible rebellion.

How did the church handle the crisis Agrippa created for the church with the capture and imprisonment of Peter? Individuals went to their family altars. In their social and public meetings, they prayed and sought the intervention of God on their behalf. The Jerusalem congregation came together for nights of prayer and intercession to God on Peter's behalf.

They knew that the weapons of their warfare were not of the flesh, that they had divine power to not only destroy strongholds but also to destroy arguments and lofty opinions raised against the knowledge of God, bringing every thought captive to obey Christ (2 Cor. 10:4–5). Intense prayer was their powerful weapon against all the wickedness and demonic strategies of the king.

Acts 12:6–10 tells the rest of the story. Shortly before Herod was about to bring him out of prison to face execution, Peter was sleeping in his cell, bound with two chains between two soldiers. Others stood guarding the door of the prison. Suddenly, an angel of the Lord stood by Peter and the prison was lit as with a bright light. The angel awoke Peter, and told him to arise quickly. As he got up, his chains fell off of his hands. The angel directed him to get dressed, put on his shoes, and to "follow me."

Peter began to follow the angel, thinking he was simply dreaming. They passed all the guards, and as they approached the iron gates of the prison, the gates suddenly opened, allowing Peter to be free and to escape death.

Intense prayer was their powerful weapon against all the wickedness and demonic strategies of the king.

Do miracles like that still happen? Yes, they do. Let me share with you the miracle that my friend Dr. Ernest Wilson and I experienced while ministering in Uganda.

Dr. Wilson and I were invited to minister at a major week-long conference of the East African Revival, held in the nation of Uganda in late January of 1977. This was a significant movement within the evangelical churches of Africa, starting in Rwanda and Burundi and spreading throughout Uganda, Tanzania, and Kenya. The revival contributed to the significant growth of the Church of England in East Africa and had a visible influence on the leaders of most denominations in those countries. Thousands of people traveled from across Uganda and from many other nations to participate in this conference.

I still remember the awesome and overwhelming sense of God's presence during the week-long meeting. It still remains the closest I've ever been to experiencing the Holy Spirit–driven realities found in the book of Acts. Daily we saw God at work: people responding to Jesus, nominal Christians repenting, people confessing their sins, believers seeking and receiving forgiveness of each other, sick bodies being prayed for and healed, and the power of God released among the people.

It was an African custom for the audience to suddenly break forth in singing, and almost every time they did they sang the same song in their language: "We praise You, Jesus, Son of the Lamb." Over and over they sang that song in recognition of the active presence of the Holy Spirit. Even during the breaks in the conferences people came up to us and greeted us with the song "We praise You Jesus, Son of the Lamb."

> *I still remember the awesome and overwhelming sense of God's presence during the week-long meeting.*

I was facilitating leadership development training in the day sessions and speaking on specific leadership and ministry subjects during the evening sessions. God's Spirit was definitely present and active among the people. Then, suddenly, something happened! On February 3 surprising news came to our host, the Rev. Dr. Joe Church, who was one of the leaders and organizers of the movement. The Revival Leadership Team was quickly assembled and a senior Ugandan church leader shared the news that Uganda's President, Idi Amin, had just declared martial law in the whole nation. "Truckloads of soldiers have been dispatched all across the country," we were told. "Some are on their way here to this conference to arrest the leaders."

President Idi Amin Dada had seized power in a military coup in 1971 and was becoming known as the "Butcher of Uganda" for his brutal, despotic rule. History now records him as possibly the most notorious of Africa's post-independence dictators. Estimates of the number of his opponents who were killed, tortured, or imprisoned vary from 100,000 to half a million.

The announcement of martial law and the dispatching of truckloads of soldiers created great consternation among the entire conference leadership. A major concern was expressed about the lives and safety of many conference organizers and specifically about the two Americans, Dr. Wilson and me.

Our British host, Dr. Joe Church, called the entire conference to prayer. He then secretly arranged for Dr. Wilson and me to get to the Entebbe International Airport immediately so as to get out of the country. We rushed to his home, picked up a few belongings, and headed off through the back streets and woods towards the airport. On our way, we saw truckloads of soldiers moving throughout Kampala the capital city. Arriving at the airport, we found it surrounded by rough-looking soldiers with their guns and bayonets drawn. The atmosphere was tense and frightening! Hundreds of families were arriving and desperately trying to find a way to leave the country.

Our hope died when we were told that all flights were canceled and that the last departing flight had already left. Everyone was in a state of desperation, confusion, and panic. Many individuals burst into tears, petrified as they saw the soldiers walking up and down the airport and staring at them as if searching for someone. Dr. Wilson and I stood there with the panic-stricken crowd. Confusion was in the air. Our driver had left, and I felt totally confused and uncertain of our next move. With all that we heard about the atrocities of President Amin, I wondered if we could possibly come out of this alive.

> *Our hope died when we were told that all flights were canceled and that the last departing flight had already left.*

I looked straight ahead of me and noticed a very tall, rough-looking soldier with his gun and bayonet. He was standing erectly, head and shoulder above the others, and looking with a keen focus in our direction. Actually, I became convinced that he was looking directly at Dr. Wilson and me. My anxiety rose; my heart began beating faster. I felt vulnerable and fearful. In a moment, it became more apparent that his eyes were on us.

A few minutes passed, and I shared with Dr. Wilson my certainty that the particular soldier was focusing on us. "Don't look now," I said, "but his eyes are on us." Then something surprising, shocking, and scary began to happen. The soldier slowly began moving in our direction. I alerted my friend. We both remained calm. I began praying in my heart, "Protect us O God. Protect us." I was now sure that the soldier was coming towards us. Closer and closer he came focusing on us. He came right to where we were standing. He then passed by my right side. I knew that he had stopped. I sensed that he had turned around and was now standing right behind us. My heart began beating even faster. My mind began to recall some of the ways Idi Amin had disposed with people he considered his enemies.

In a split second, the soldier tightly grabbed my left upper arm and pushed me forward. As I lurched forward, I noticed that Dr. Wilson did as well. The soldier was tightly squeezing our arms and pushing both of us forward. Not a word was uttered. Not a sound was made. We couldn't look back. His grasp was firm, and he continued to squeeze our arms and push us right through the anxious and petrified crowd—past the other soldiers, past the ticket counters, straight to the back doorway. He pushed us out through the boarding door of the airport and outside, onto the tarmac. He forcibly kept pushing us without a word.

His grip was firm, strong, rigid, and tightening. I was struck with panic and felt a sense of consternation. There was no use trying to resist. I remember wondering, "Where is he taking us? Will I ever see my family again? How will our wives and families know what really happened to us?"

It was a long walk—more like a long push. Nothing was in front of us, and no airplanes were on the runway. Then he pushed us around a turn. One airplane was parked way off in the distance. I thought, "He must be pushing us towards that airplane. Whose plane is that? Why is he pushing us there? Is that a military airplane?" Where will it take us? Who else is on it?"

In a split second, the soldier tightly grabbed my left upper arm and pushed me forward.

He did not speak a single word as he continued pushing us the full distance right to that airplane. I was petrified! My sense of danger and panic became more intense. He pushed us to the first step of the airplane, then up the second and third steps. Then he shocked us when he shouted the words of the song we had been singing all through the conference: "We praise You Jesus, Son of the Lamb."

"Ah!" I gasped, "He must be a believer. Is he rescuing us?" Baffled and somewhat relieved, both Dr. Wilson and I immediately turned around to see the person and to say thank you. We were stunned—there was no one there! We both looked at the distance over which we had been pushed. There was no one there. We looked at each other in utter amazement, pondering what we had just experienced.

We stepped into the airplane, took the only two seats that were empty, and put on our seat belts. We had not approached the ticket counter at the airport, nor had we any opportunity to present our travel documents or passports, yet we were now in our seats on the airplane.

Immediately, the pilot announced, "We have finally been released for departure." We asked those around us, "Has anyone seen the person who brought us to the plane?" No one saw anyone with us—neither the attendants nor the passengers. They said that no one accompanied us as we arrived at the plane. At this moment we realized with certainty that God had sent a tall, strong, male African angel to push us out of Uganda and deliver us from the plans of Idi Amin.

The airplane took off, with many of the passengers expressing anger because they felt we had held up the plane for hours while they were sweating in the tropical heat without any air conditioning. They knew nothing about the fact that martial law had been declared or about the truckloads of soldiers who were surrounding and had taken possession of the airport. Others were quite curious, inquiring, "Who are these two special people that the plane had to wait hours just for them?"

"Who are these two special people that the plane had to wait hours just for them?"

In Acts chapter 12, God sent an angel to deliver Peter from the hand of King Herod Agrippa. That day at the Entebbe International Airport in Uganda, God sent a tall, dark, male African angel to deliver Dr. Wilson and me from the hands of President Idi Amin. Why did God deliver Peter and later us? Only He knows. We traveled back to Philadelphia via London, like Mary, pondering these things in our hearts.

My supernatural push and deliverance out of Uganda also pushed me into a new consciousness of the interventions of the Holy Spirit and the awesome realization that God is concerned about me and the future He has for my life. I am sure that you have heard the statement, "God doesn't always come, but He sends." That statement is not true. For God to be unable to come and just send someone else suggests that He is busy or otherwise occupied with something much more important. God always comes even in the people he uses to meet our needs. Delivering us was another significant investment of God in us. Every day I live, I am conscious of that great day of divine intervention and deliverance.

Wisdom for Living

1. What guidance would you give to a person on how to handle a major crisis?
2. What experience have you had that gave you the confidence of God's presence?
3. How do think we felt when we came to the realization that God actually sent an angel to deliver us?
4. Do you believe that God still sends angels to help us today?

Chapter 13

The Archbishop Who Was Killed by Idi Amin after We Escaped

It was terrible shock to arrive back in the United States and discover that my friend, Archbishop Janani Jakaliya Luwum of the Church of Uganda, one of the most influential leaders of the modern church in Africa, and with whom I had tea just two days earlier, had been arrested and killed by Ugandan President Idi Amin's orders. His execution was motivated by the president's anger about the East African Christian Leadership Conference as well as the fact that Dr. Ernest Wilson and I had obviously escaped and left the country.

The church in Uganda began with the deaths of martyrs. Around 1900, Uganda became a British protectorate, with the chief of the Buganda tribe as nominal ruler, and with several other tribes included in the protectorate. In 1962 Uganda became an independent country within the British Commonwealth, with the Bugandan chief as president and Milton Obote, of the Lango tribe, as Prime Minister. In 1966, Obote took full control of the government.

In 1971, he was overthrown by General Idi Amin, Chief of Staff of the Armed Forces. Almost immediately, Idi Amin began a policy of repression, arresting anyone suspected of not supporting him. Hundreds of soldiers from the Lango and Acholi tribes were shot down in their barracks. Over the next few years, many Christians were killed for various offenses. A preacher was shot in 1972 for reading over the radio a passage from the Psalms that mentioned Israel. Early in 1977, President Idi Amin was determined to stamp out all traces of dissent. His men killed thousands, including the entire population of Milton Obote's home village.

Early in 1977, President Idi Amin was determined to stamp out all traces of dissent.

On Sunday, January 30th, my friend Bishop Festo Kivengere preached on "The Preciousness of Life" to an audience that included many high government officials. He denounced the arbitrary bloodshed, and accused the government of abusing the authority that God had entrusted to it. President

Idi Amin became upset that Bishop Kivengere, Dr. Ernest Wilson, and I were allowed in the country and were sharing in the leadership of the major leadership conference.

The government responded on Saturday, February 5th with an early-morning (1:30 a.m.) raid of the home of Archbishop Janani Luwum, ostensibly to search for hidden stores of weapons. Amin accused the archbishop of treason, produced a bogus document supposedly by former President Obote attesting to his guilt, and had the archbishop and two cabinet members (both committed Christians) arrested and held for military trial. The three met briefly with four other prisoners who were awaiting execution and were permitted to pray with them briefly. Then the three were placed in a Land Rover and never seen alive again.

The government story is that one of the prisoners tried to seize control of the vehicle, that it was wrecked, and the passengers killed. The archbishop's body was placed in a sealed coffin and sent to his native village for burial. Suspicious of the government's version of events, the villagers opened the coffin and discovered bullet holes in the body. The archbishop's supporters believe that he refused to sign a confession, was beaten and otherwise abused, and finally shot.

In the capital city of Kampala, a crowd of about 4,500 gathered for a memorial service beside the grave that had been prepared for him next to that of the martyred Bishop Hannington. In Nairobi, the capital of nearby Kenya, about 10,000 gathered for another memorial service. Bishop Kivengere was informed that he was about to be arrested, so he and his family fled to Kenya, as did the widow and orphans of Archbishop Luwum.

Suspicious of the government's version of events, the villagers opened the coffin and discovered bullet holes in the body.

The following June, about 25,000 Ugandans came to the capital to celebrate the centennial of the first preaching of the gospel in their country. Among the participants were many who had abandoned Christianity, but had returned to their faith as a result of seeing the courage of Archbishop Luwum and his companions in the face of death.

When Dr. Wilson and I had tea with Archbishop Luwum at his home two days before we escaped Uganda and several days before he was killed, it was clear to me that here was a man of faith. His faith had been severely tested, and he was anchored. Archibishop Luwan echoed a thought Bishop Desmond Tutu had expressed: "A life of wholeness does not depend on what we experience. Wholeness depends on how we experience our lives."[17] He understood that if our faith is not tested, it cannot be trusted. He did not see the life of faith as a process of simply mounting up with wings as eagles, but also a life of daily walking, trusting God, and not fainting. His various experiences with God, developed in him a settled faith grounded in God's absolute infallibility.

The archbishop had a unique perception of the grace of God. Not knowing that he would be put to death by President Idi Amin just a few days later, he saw God's grace as a means of divine influence that is seen only by its effects. We cannot see life except in its effects. We see the nature of a tree not simply by looking at the tree itself, but by the leaves and fruits it produces. Even so, the archbishop felt that living in God's grace meant reaching the place where one's total life reflects the influence and consciousness of that inner divine deposit and strength. His inner spiritual consciousness and peace were manifested just a few days later when he was captured and killed by Idi Amin.

The Church of England honored him by erecting a statue of him, along with two other martyred saints, at one of the entrances of the West Minister Abby in London England.

He understood that if our faith is
not tested, it cannot be trusted.

Wisdom for Living

1. Idi Amin's government reported that a prisoner tried to seize control of a vehicle in which the archbishop was riding, resulting in a wreck that killed the archbishop and other passengers. When returned to his people for burial, they opened the coffin and saw bullet holes in his body. Why is it important that leaders be held to the highest standard of truth?

2. What does it mean to be faithful to God even in the face of death?

3. Why do you think God's church always grows and gets stronger under persecution?

4. Think of some major trials you have experienced. What did you learn from them, and how did they make your faith grow?

Chapter 14

The News That Our Baby Was Dead

We were quite comfortable with three children when my wife discovered that she was pregnant. We were not planning for such an event. Imagine her emotions when she later received the mind-boggling news that she was carrying twins. We did not know the genders, so we picked out some possible names, one for a boy and one for a girl.

This led to a time of great testing of our faith that resulted in one of the greatest miracles of our lives. Since my wife was the one who was pregnant, I have asked her to recount this particular significant experience for you.

Hyacinth's Story

My labor began around lunchtime on October 14, 1980. I had a very large and successful party-plan distributorship, and I remember rushing to get my orders in by noon and thanking God that I had succeeded in that task, when I became aware that my water had broken. A quick call to my ob-gyn doctor confirmed my suspicion that labor had begun.

For several hours, I "labored" indeed (excuse the pun), then, totally exhausted, I finally left everything to God. The particular doctor assigned to me was the youngest, newest, and most recent member of the obstetrics team, and he was most anxious to deliver the twins—his first, he said.

The contractions were prolonged and finally got weaker. However, so much time had elapsed that it was time for this young doctor to leave and for my favorite doctor to take over. Within a relatively short period, I was ready to be wheeled into the OR, which was a beehive of activity. Two sets of personnel were prepared to take care of baby #1 and baby #2.

My husband was there, capped and gowned like the other professionals. He had a camera in his hands that he intended to use to his advantage. The doctor in charge had prepped me for an epidural because twins are unpredictable.

The excitement in the delivery room rose sharply as baby #1 quickly made his appearance, and Andrew Stanley Grannum was born. My husband, standing at my shoulder, was able to take a full shot of him as the doctor held him up. The baby's team sprang into action. We named him Andrew based on John 1:40–43. Just as the discipleAndrew had led his brother Peter to Jesus, in a sense, baby #1 had led baby #2 into this world.

Now the team for baby #2 took its position. The doctor began to look somewhat anxious, then obviously worried as he said, "I can't quite locate baby #2. Where is he hiding?"

Looking even more worried, he ordered, "Get the monitor!" and almost instantaneously I was hooked up to it. All eyes turned to watch the screen; a deep hush fell on everyone as we saw the flat line. Even lay persons like my husband and I knew what that meant. Wordlessly, the team for baby #2 filed out of the room, which suddenly seemed very dark, with the atmosphere of a funeral.

The doctor came to the head of the table to talk to me. "Hyacinth, your baby is in trouble, but we have to get him out."

I asked him, "You think he is dead, don't you?"

He replied, "Yes, but we still have to get him out. I will do an emergency cesarean on you. Luckily, we had prepared you for the surgery just in case something happened."

I closed my eyes and said to the Lord, "Lord, I never asked you for twins. You told me that you were giving me twins, and I sure never asked you for a dead baby." By the time that tearful statement had been made in my mind and spirit, a gas mask was put on my face, and I was unconscious.

My husband told me that at that point he began to pray earnestly to God for the life of this child. It was serious and focused intercession, an intense stretching of faith and believing for a miracle as he watched the struggle the doctor was experiencing.

The doctor began to look somewhat anxious, then obviously worried.

The doctor told us afterward that he had a most difficult decision to make about where to make the incision and on which part of the baby he would first place his hands. We believe that the Lord led him to make the incision in the right place to access the child whose position was quite high and who had his umbilical cord wrapped around his neck. My husband said the baby's coloring was quite different from that of his brother. The doctor consoled him by saying, "Mr. Grannum, you have at least one healthy baby. I am very sorry. The other baby was definitely without oxygen for too long."

Baby #2 was brought out, placed on a table, and pretty much ignored. My husband looked at that motionless blue baby and began to pray again. "O God, you are the giver of life. You could give life to this child." He continued stretching his faith and believing God for a miracle.

> *"Mr. Grannum, you have at least*
> *one healthy baby. I am very sorry.*
> *The other baby was definitely*
> *without oxygen for too long."*

My husband later told me that after a long while, the nurse who had remained in the room glanced at the dead child on the table, took a second glance, and suddenly exclaimed, "This baby just moved. I'm sure if it." She rushed out of the room making the announcement in the hearing of the doctor and team that had left. Immediately the doctor and some members of the team for baby #2 rushed back. The doctor picked up the baby, gave him a few customary "smacks" and worked on him until the child gave a feeble cry. The doctor in amazement began to examine the child then spoke to him. "Mr. Grannum, this child will have severe a brain injury, but at least he's alive."

When he heard that, he lifted his eyes and heart to the same God who had just performed a miracle by giving life to our son. The pronouncement that the child would have severe a brain injury made his heart very heavy. He began to pray again and ask God for a second miracle.

It was then that God gave him the name for the baby, Samuel Grannum. (Samuel means "gift from God.") In the Bible, the baby Samuel's birth was an answered prayer. When I awoke and was given all the details, I too felt that the name Samuel was a reflection of the fact that God is good. He "is able to do exceedingly abundantly above all that we ask or think" (Eph. 3:20, NKJV).

Sometime later, the first doctor who had to leave before the delivery heard about all that happened. He said to us, "I am so glad that my time ran out and I had to leave, because this would have been my first delivery of twins, and I would not have known what to do under those circumstances." His statement showed us that God had orchestrated this delivery, because He already knew that the umbilical cord was wrapped around Samuel's neck.

What about the Idea of His Being Severely Brain Damaged?

We continued to commit our son to the Lord and watched as Samuel grew up, committed his life to the Lord, and went on to enjoy participating in a vast array of sports. His athletic ability, his height, strength, and size caused him to be a stand-out in football, basketball, track and field, and cross country. Samuel achieved honors and recognition for his outstanding play as the starting center in basketball at his high school. He graduated from Cheltenham High School in 1999 as the all-time shot blocker in the school's history, a title he held for nine years.

After only one season of playing basketball at the high school varsity level, he received a full scholarship to play Division I basketball from the University of Maryland, Baltimore County.

> *He began to pray again and ask*
> *God for a second miracle.*

Later, he transferred to West Chester University in Pennsylvania. During his three seasons there, West Chester University's men's basketball team achieved record-breaking distinction. The team had an 11-game winning streak, which still stands as a school record, and reached a national ranking of number 11 in the United States in Division II. Sam broke West Chester University's shot blocking record for a single season, recording seventy-eight blocks, and finally finished his career as the all-time shot blocker in West Chester University's history. All three records still stand today.

In 2008, as part of his desire for missions, Sam began conducting basketball clinics in Guyana, South America, with the Elite 24, Guyana's junior national basketball team.

In March of 2015, he founded the Sports and Mentoring Student Community (SAMS Community) in Philadelphia. This program is designed to enhance the social, emotional, physical, and personal development of youth ages twelve to eighteen and establish a sense of community stewardship through service learning, social life skills workshops, academic enrichment, tutoring, and physical fitness.

Sam now serves as the chief operations officer of the almost forty-acre campus of the New Covenant Church of Philadelphia. He is responsible for the daily operations, management, marketing, development, and funding of all New Covenant campus departments as well as the economic development initiatives of all New Covenant corporations, both for-profit and not-for-profit.

In March of 2015, he founded the Sports and Mentoring Student Community (SAMS Community) in Philadelphia.

Wisdom for Living

1. How does Sam's story reflect his parents' faith in God?
2. Due to the slow birthing process, the first attending doctor had to leave before he could deliver his first set of twins. What does this incident reveal about God?
3. God responded when we rejected the report of a dead baby. How and what do you think about this?

4. What is the evidence that God contradicted the doctor's assessment of the child having a severe brain injury?

5. What are some of the areas your life for which you can develop faith and begin to trust God today?

Chapter 15

Spiritual Wisdom I Gained from an Aged African Preacher

He was a man with only a third-grade education, but he significantly impacted my life with his wisdom and sensitivity. In February of 1977 I was introduced to him while I was a guest speaker at the East African Revival Leadership Conference in Uganda.

He was a very old and highly respected leader. I was told that he traveled hundreds of miles each year on his bicycle to visit the many congregations for which he gave oversight. I was impressed by his age, stamina, alertness, and unbelievable wisdom. He had very little formal education, but it was obvious that he had spent many years learning by sitting at the feet of Jesus.

I was one of the speakers invited from the US; I was a college and seminary graduate. At that time, I had earned a doctor of education degree and a doctor of philosophy, both with academic honors. My picture, biographic sketch, and degrees were on the flyers, and people sat and listened to me with a sense of expectancy.

However, while fellowshipping with this old leader with only a third-grade education, it wasn't very long before I realized that I had earned the academic degrees, but he had captured the wisdom and power of the Holy Spirit, far beyond my experience. Conscious of his wisdom, I ask him a question. "My brother, how would you define spiritual depth or spiritual maturity?" I personally thought that was a very deep question.

Without much hesitation, he replied, "Oh, brother, that's very simple. Spiritual depth or spiritual maturity simply means reaching the place in your life where you can actually see people and circumstances through the eyes of Jesus."

Wow! Unbelievable! I doubt if my university or seminary professors would have captured it and explained it that clearly. His response was almost without thought. His answer did not come from books in a library. It came from his heart and his spending time with God. Over the decades, I continue to reflect on his wisdom, discernment, insight, and clarity of revelation. "Spiritual depth or spiritual maturity simply means reaching the place in your life where you can actually see people and circumstances through the eyes of Jesus."

*Over the decades, I continue to
reflect on his wisdom, discernment,
insight and clarity of revelation.*

Both you and I know that we can look at people, smile, shake their hands and yet not really see them. That may sound contradictory, but we can see, yet not see. Hear what God says to Ezekiel: "My people have eyes to see but do not see, and ears to hear but do not hear" (Ezek. 12:2). The Bible has a very interesting word for really seeing. It is the word "behold." Beholding is not merely seeing. It is seeing with an intensity and insight that goes beyond a mere physical processing of light, things or people entering the eye.

When Jesus healed a blind man, he asked him, "Do you see anything?" The man replied, "I see men as trees walking." He could see, but he was confused. Jesus touched his eyes again, and he saw clearly. He had not only sight, but *insight*, to make sense of what he saw (Mark 8:22–26). By touching the man a second time, Jesus was indicating that it was not enough to see. The blind man was now seeing. He did have sight, but Jesus went further by asking him what specifically was he seeing. Based on his answer, Jesus touched him again so that he could see people clearly.

Seeing people through the eyes of Jesus is far more than simply the ability to see people. It goes beyond mere human sight to spiritual insight. Seeing without insight is seeing without understanding, without discerning, without significance—and that is not really seeing at a deep level.

For the growing Christian, disciplining oneself and learning to see people through the eyes of Jesus is the most important kind of seeing. That is indeed capturing spiritual reality. People's physical eye could be clear to certain outward things, but their inward eye is blind, thus leaving their view of people and this world rather faulty.

One of the important benefits of seeking, praying, and disciplining ourselves to see people through the eyes of Jesus is that it helps us to see ourselves more clearly. It also helps us to have a deeper insight into God's plan for our lives.

The apostle Paul put this way: "I pray that the eyes of your heart may be enlightened in order that you may know the hope to which he [God] has called you, the riches of his glorious inheritance in his holy people" (Ephesians 1:18, NIV).

Everybody needs to see something deeper and experience new ideas about life and living. There are things that you and I do today in very normal and natural ways, and yet a deeper insight would enable us to perceive differently, act differently, and respond to people, circumstances, and life in general differently. This is one of the most powerful principles of life. We never know what could be done until we see things with different eyes. New vision and insights enable us to take the risk of doing something we have never done before

To disregard this effort and to refuse to see deeper and take risks is to exist without ever experiencing the joy and the power of creative and spiritual living.

We never know what could be done
until we see things with different eyes.

Ask God daily to help you capture the insight of seeing people and circumstances through the eyes of Jesus.

Wisdom for Living

1. My question to the aged preacher was, "My brother, how would you explain a person's striving for spiritual depth or spiritual maturity?" How would you have answered that?

2. Remember his response? "Oh, brother, that's very simple. Spiritual depth or spiritual maturity simply means reaching the place in your life where you can actually see people and circumstances through the eyes of Jesus." What do you gain from that?

3. What does that answer reveal about the nature of his life, ministry, and sensitivity to God?

4. How do you think it influenced his relationship with his family?

Chapter 16

The Risk an Eminent Physician Took with Me

My son, pay attention to my wisdom; Lend your ear to my understanding.

Proverbs 5:1, NKJV

I had been preaching even before I was a teenager, but in 1982 I developed a problem with my throat, partly due to many years of hard preaching without a microphone. At this time, I was pastoring the High Street Church of God at 222 East High Street in Philadelphia, Pennsylvania.

One of the members of the church recommended her doctor to me. Dr. Albert Seltzer was an eminent ear, nose, and throat specialist. He always booked me as his patient so that we could talk about religious subjects following my examinations. One day we were in his office talking, and he asked me a question that was different from any he had asked me before. "Doctor Grannum, do you ever take opportunities to travel to watch great preachers operate?"

Of course, he used the word "operate" because that was his natural vocabulary as a surgeon. When I think of preachers, I think of them ministering or leading or developing their vision. However, I responded to this question. "No, my friend. I am usually in my church on Sundays except those times when I am away fulfilling speaking engagements."

He looked at me very sadly, then remarked. "Doctor, you are good, actually, you are very good. I listen to your tapes and I sometimes catch many of your nightly radio programs. You are good! But you will never be great until you take the time to travel and see how really great preachers operate."

He then said, "When I was in medical school my father, a medical doctor, said to me, 'Son, when you are reading articles in the American medical journal, and you come across information on a specialist who is doing something significant anywhere in the country, call that person, tell him or her what you are reading, and ask if you can come to his or her city for one day just to watch him or her operate.' I started and continue doing it, and I have never had a physician say no to my request."

In his concluding words to me he repeated what he had said before: "You are very good, but you will never be great until you take the time to travel and see how really great preachers operate." In that moment, on that day, he taught me a significant lesson about life and the importance of exposure.

*"You will never be great until you
take the time to travel and see how
really great preachers operate."*

Sometime after that, my wife and I spent two weeks in California, talking with pastors of different denominations and their leaders, paying special attention to their processes, legal and administrative structures, ministries, and accomplishments. We picked their brains on a number of areas and began to see some common denominators emerging from their responses. Our eyes opened wider and wider as we listened and captured the many processes through which they were able to handle their challenges and turn their water into wine.

We returned to Philadelphia, having captured some new insights into the statement Jesus made in John 3:11: "Truly, truly, I say to you, we speak of what we know, and bear witness to what we have seen." Since we testify only what we have seen, our testimony and communication to any point is based on only our past exposure and experiences. In order to expand our insights and testimony, we must decide to see more, to expose ourselves to new experiences that are far beyond the normal.

My wife and I realized that, in order to grow and move beyond our urrent experiences and productivity, we needed to constantly expose ourselves to other ministries and other ministers, seeing more and knowing more about what God is doing in other places.

Dr. Seltzer's advice was an enhancing moment and an instrument that placed my wife and me on a new journey of personal and ministry growth and development. He was clear and did not beat around the bush. He did not feel the need to be diplomatic. There were many evenings when he listened to my radio program *Wisdom from the Word*. He envisioned the potential of my program and my ministry. As a result, he decided to push me in a direction necessary for further development.

To this point I had been ministering for a number of years. I had traveled from Guyana to Trinadad, back to Guyana, then to the US, and I was having what I considered to be a successful ministry as pastor of the High Street Church of God in Philadelphia. Things were going well. Yet in all of that, I had assumed that developing a *good* ministry was enough. I had never been challenged to truly focus on and intentionally examine the fundamental principles of developing a truly *great* ministry.

What medical doctor can become a great surgeon without ever being in classes and operating rooms, studying surgeons performing their surgical procedures? All great professionals at some point became understudies of more experienced professionals. Can you imagine an engineer taking charge of a team to build a bridge across a major stream, when that engineer had never been part of such a team before?

> *Yet in all of that, I had assumed that developing a good ministry was enough.*

One of our daughters-in-law loves cake making and cake decorating. She is very good at what she does and loves. Yet she is continually in classes with other people of similar interests, led by expert bakers—people who not only have an interest in cake making and decorating, but the proven skills and experience necessary to train others. Another one of our sons and his wife are developing an innovative business, which also requires capturing deeper experiences in that field.

While many pastors and other spiritual leaders are trained and expected to focus only on practices and organizational leadership within their denominations, greater wisdom would suggest that we be pushed to expose our minds to new ideas, to stretch our vision, and learn from other skillful master leaders in our respective fields of endeavor. Dr. Seltzer helped my wife and me to begin the practice of doing that.

While many pastors and other spiritual leaders are trained and expected to focus only on practices and organizational leadership within their denominations, greater wisdom would suggest that we be pushed to expose our minds to new ideas.

Dr. Seltzer has now passed on, but my heart is filled with gratitude to him for the risk he took in pushing me to toward greater exposure and vision. His advice could very well have been seen as threatening to me. Embracing such empowering moments, however, can change the outcome of any given situation. Many people strive daily to better them-selves, knowing that even the smallest improvements can make a bigger impact on their own lives and those around them. That day, the risk Dr. Seltzer took with me continues to positively enhance my life.

Wisdom for Living

1. How would you have really felt if Dr. Albert Seltzer had told you, "You are good, actually, you are very good. But you will never be great until you take the time to travel and see how really great leaders operate"?
2. What do you think were his real intentions?
3. Why do you think he chose to take the risk?
4. What do you think are some of the ways I could have reacted to his statement?
5. How did I interpret both his statement and his motives and benefit from them?

Chapter 17

Imagine—A Blind Woman with Leprosy, in Full-time Ministry!

I cannot remember how I became aware of the leprosy hospital and began ministering to the patients there, but it became the background to one of the most significant encounters of my life.

During my teenage years, our youth ministry team visited and attended to poor and homeless patients of Hindu Pandit Ramsaroop Marajh's Darm Shala, a home for the aged and sick. We also ministered on a regular basis at a geriatric institution for sick, crippled, mentally ill, and neglected adults called the Georgetown PALMS (also known as the Alms House), a geriatric institution located in Brickdam.[18] This was the final home for thousands of our senior citizens. We also held regular ministry to the residents of the Archer Poor House, a residence for many elderly and less fortunate people in Georgetown, Guyana.

Years later, during my early pastoral ministry, I continued the tradition by traveling to the village of Mahaica on a monthly basis to minister to the patients at a leper hospital. This Roman Catholic institution has a colorful history.

In 1933 (when Guyana was known as British Guiana), members of the Sisters of the Immaculate Conception traveled from Moravia, Czechoslovakia, to Mahaica with a burden to care for the large number of patients at the Mahaica Leprosarium, as it was then called. (Leprosy was, and to some extent still is, considered a dreaded disease.) The Moravian nuns were later joined by several members of the Sisters of Mercy, who assumed charge of the hospital. They dedicated more than thirty-five years of their lives in faithful service to the patients in this unique, totally isolated, and almost abandoned community.

As infectious diseases go, leprosy is still one of the most misunderstood. As a result of the many popular misconceptions about this dreadful disease, those suffering from it were generally considered outcasts and relegated to neglected margins of urban centers. For some reason, these suffering and isolated people were close to my heart, and I really enjoyed the times I spent ministering to them. I would lead them in singing hymns of their choice, allow them to share memorized Scripture passages, and even allow them to give short talks about their lives. The time I spent with them gave me insights into their life circumstances and significantly influenced my life journey and ministry.

I will never forget the impact of the final worship service I had with them. When they discovered that it was going to be our last service together because I was leaving the country, they all cried, and so did I. However, there was one person who attended regularly and was not present.

Her name was Rose.

I asked the others where Rose was, and learned that she

As infectious diseases go, leprosy is still one of the most misunderstood.

was not well. At that moment, I knew that I could not simply send a goodbye message to Rose; I could not leave that institution without seeing her.

I went into the ward and found her on her bed. Leprosy had destroyed her vision; it had eaten off parts of both her hands and legs, and left the rest of her skin thickened, wrinkled, and discolored. I stood there, watching mosquitos biting her and seeing the blood running down stumps of what used to be her arms. All she could do was flinch and shake her body.

As I approached her bed, I began to softly sing one of her favorite hymns, written by another blind woman, Fanny Crosby:

> Jesus, keep me near the cross:
> There a precious fountain.
> Free to all, a healing stream,
> Flows from Calvary's mountain.

In the cross, in the cross
Be my glory ever,
Till my raptured soul shall find
Rest beyond the river.[19]

When she heard my singing she broke out with a wide smile. "It's got to be you, Pastor."

I sang all of the verses of the hymn to her and then informed her that I was leaving the country and would most likely never see her again. She straightened up, became perfectly still as if shocked. She stared in my direction, though she had no eyes to see me. Tears began to flow. I couldn't hug her, kiss her, or even touch her. My tears began to flow as well. Softly, I continued humming that favorite hymn. "Jesus keep me near the cross."

> *When she heard my singing she broke out with a wide smile. "It's got to be you, Pastor."*

Then it happened! Rose made an extremely difficult request of me. It significantly impacted me and continues to impact me to this day.

"Pastor, since you're leaving, and I may never in this life see you again, would you do me a special favor?"

"Certainly Rose, I would be happy to do it if I can."

Her response surprised and shocked me.

"Pastor, since you're leaving and I may never in this life see you again, would you pray a special prayer for me, please?" She saw me as her pastor, and it was natural for her to ask me to pray for her, but the request, on that day, and at that moment, unnerved me.

I had served and led in my home church since I was eleven or twelve years old. I had led prayer meetings, done street meetings, and preached for revival services as a teenager. I was now serving as the pastor of two churches in the city. In Trinidad, I had studied theology and pastoral ministry for four years and had also pastored a church there. Yet at that moment, it was as if Rose had asked me to perform an absolutely impossible task. It seemed like a task for which none of my experiences had adequately prepared me.

I was floored because I considered this a really special and serious request, and I didn't want to offer up a generic prayer. It was important to me that my prayer for this woman, who had no eyes, no hands, and no feet, should give her hope and encourage her to continue living a purposeful and fulfilled life.

In an attempt to capture my composure, I asked, "Rose, what exactly do you want me to pray for?" I needed her to tell me, because I didn't know what to ask God for, in light of her condition. Smiling, she said, "Well, Pastor, my prayer is always the same and very simple. Ask God that as I sit on this bed every day with my sickness of leprosy, no eyes, no arms, no legs, no money, no family, with high blood pressure and diabetes, ask God to help me each day to show the nurses and doctors that I am a Christian. That's all I want. That's all I want God to do."

I was blown away! Her only focus was on ministry to those around her, who were taking care of her. It is difficult to imagine being in that position—incurable leprosy, arms and legs eaten off by the disease, totally blind, high blood pressure, diabetes, no family, no money and sitting on a bed day after day. It was impossible for her to take care of her physical needs without assistance. What would your prayer have been? Might it not in some ways have reflected the old song, "Nobody Knows the Trouble I've Seen"?

"Rose, what exactly do you want me to pray for?"

How amazing it is that Rose, who was bedridden, saw herself in full-time ministry and happily did what she could for God. Her ministry purpose was to ensure that those around her and those taking care of her would see that she was a Christian. This reflected supernatural anointing and commitment to her life mission. Her faith in God was so settled that she did not allow her sickness and her physical challenges to cause her to be offended at what God had allowed in her life.

Sitting on her bed they after day with leprosy, blind, no arms, no legs, high blood pressure and diabetes, unable to even go to the bathroom on her own, Rose was committed to being a full-time missionary for God. She knew what she really wanted.

What you and I really want totally defines us. It is the most fundamental question of our Christian lives as disciples of Jesus. When the two disciples of John the Baptist came to check out Jesus on John's request, Jesus' first question to them was "What do you want?" (John 1:38). Our lives are not determined by what we believe, what we know, what we think, or even how we feel, but by what we really want deep down in our hearts. This is the core of our being and identity.

Rose's vision of herself was not determined by her condition. Sitting on that bed daily without eyes, legs, or arms and with leprosy did not determine her sense of who she was. She knew who she was because she knew what she wanted to be, a missionary for Jesus.

Here is my question to you: What do *you* really want?

Luke 7:23 states, "And blessed is the one who is not offended by me." What is the context of this passage? It is found in Matthew 4:12–14: "Now when he heard that John had been arrested, he withdrew into Galilee. And leaving Nazareth he went and lived in Capernaum by the sea, in the territory of Zebulun and Naphtali, so that what was spoken by the prophet Isaiah might be fulfilled."

> ### *Rose's vision of herself was not determined by her condition.*

In this passage, John the Baptist is in prison and after a while he becomes concerned about whether or not Jesus whom he presented to the world is really the Christ that Isaiah spoke about. It was quite natural for John to have expected that Jesus would perform some miraculous act that would cause him to be released from prison, especially since he had heard about all the wonderful things that Jesus was doing. Luke 7:18–23 says,

> The disciples of John reported all these things
> to him. And John, calling two of his disciples

to him, sent them to the Lord, saying, "Are
you the one who is to come, or shall we look
for another?" And when the men had come
to him, they said, "John the Baptist has sent
us to you, saying, 'Are you the one who is
to come, or shall we look for another?'" In
that hour he healed many people of diseases
and plagues and evil spirits, and on many
who were blind he bestowed sight. And he
answered them, "Go and tell John what you
have seen and heard: the blind receive their
sight, the lame walk, lepers are cleansed, and
the deaf hear, the dead are raised up, the
poor have good news preached to them. And
blessed is the one who is not offended by me."

In life, you will find that there are those who are offended
by the things that God has allowed into their lives, and there
are those like Rose, who choose to live their lives in a happy
pursuit of their purpose.

Rose's spirit definitely differed from that of a former member of the High Street church I once pastored in Philadelphia.
This young man had tremendous promise but was struggling
with cancer. He would come to church and prayer meetings as
he dealt with his illness, but as time went by, he became bitter
and removed himself from the church.

My wife and I distinctly remember the evening our
phone rang, and all we could hear was a neighbor of the
church shouting, "Pastor, the church is on fire!" We were
shocked—stunned with disbelief. We hurriedly got out of

bed, got dressed quickly, jumped into our car and sped toward the church. As we approached, we could see the redness of the fire reflecting off the clouds and smell the smoke. By the time the fire was put out, a major part of our church's parish hall was destroyed.

"Pastor, the church is on fire!"

Fires were also set at three different churches in Philadelphia over the following days. Some time later, it came to my attention who had set fire to our church. It was the young man dealing with cancer, the former member who had attended prayer meetings seeking healing but not receiving it. It seems that after a while he took up an offensive against God and the church, and setting fires to churches was his way of demonstrating and dealing with his feelings. Even after I was informed, I chose not to tell the police. Instead, I committed him to God. His health continued to deteriorate, and after some time he died.

It would have been so easy for Rose in her sickness and helplessness to have been offended by God. She could have questioned God by asking, "Why me?" Instead, she chose to be at peace because she understood that, in spite of her circumstances, she could still fulfill her purpose, which was to use her life to show Christ to others.

Rose reminded me of Charles Naylor, one of the early pioneers of the Church of God. Born in southern Ohio in 1874, he became part of the church at age nineteen and was ordained in 1899 in Springfield, Ohio. In 1908 he suffered a dislocated kidney and other internal injuries while moving timbers from under a camp meeting tent. A year later he was involved in a bus accident that caused him to be an invalid for the rest of his life. In that condition, he not only served as a columnist for the *Gospel Trumpet* magazine, but also authored eight books and many articles, pamphlets, hymns, and gospel songs. Below is one of the hymns he wrote in 1902:[20]

I Am the Lord's
Whether I live or die, Whether I wake or sleep,
Whether upon the land, Or on the stormy deep;
When 'tis serene and calm, Or when the wild winds blow,
I shall not be afraid—I am the Lord's, I know.

When with abundant store, Or in deep poverty,
When all the world may smile,
Or it may frown on me;
When it shall help me on, Or shall obstruct my way,
Still shall my heart rejoice—I
am the Lord's today.

When I am safe at home, Or in a foreign land,
When on an icebound shore,
Or on a sunlit strand;
When on the mountain height, Or in the valley low,
Still doth He care for me— I
am the Lord's, I know.

Nothing shall separate From His unbounded love,
Neither in depths below, Nor
in the heights above;

And in the years to come, He will abide with me;
I am the Lord's indeed, For all eternity.

Whenever I think of Rose and the impact she's had in my life and the lives of so many, I think of the story in John 2 where Jesus went to the wedding, was confronted with a need and ended up turning water into wine. This is what Rose was doing every day. From her bed, confronted with her realities, she was quietly allowing her light to shine and turning her bitter water into wine.

She could have questioned God by asking, "Why me?" Instead, she chose to be at peace

Wisdom for Living

1. Why do you feel that I needed to see Rose before I left?
2. Visualize and describe Rose and her condition to someone.
3. How would you have managed sitting on the bed each day with leprosy, with no feet, no arms and no eyes?
4. If the pastor had come to see you for the last time, what would've been your prayer request?
5. How do you explain Rose's daily commitment to spend the rest of her life being a missionary for God to others?

6. Why do you think that John the Baptist sent his disciples to verify that Jesus was indeed the Christ?
7. What are some of the reasons why people tend to get offended by God?

Chapter 18

Everybody Gets a Push—Learn to Benefit from Yours

*Do not pray for easy lives! Pray to be stronger
men and women. Do not pray for tasks equal to
your powers. Pray for powers equal to your tasks.
Then the doing of your work shall be no miracle,
but you shall be a miracle.*

—Phillips Brooks (1835–1893)

S ometimes I sit and reflect on all of the physical, mental, and emotional abuse I experienced and wonder what my mother really expected to accomplish. I am sure she felt she would finally bring me to my senses and help me to become as settled as she thought my four older brothers were. After all, I was the youngest and not seen to be as wise as they were.

All of my brothers, who at the time really had no interest in God and church, were assisted by one of our aunts to travel from Guyana to England to better themselves. I, on the other hand, was pushed out of my home because of my commitment to a church that was perceived to have no meaningful future for me. The pain of that event eventually helped me make some significant decisions and discoveries about life.

After a number of years, efforts, and experiences, I discovered that the true meaning and magic of life does not emerge while one lives simply in the active pursuit of comfort. Many people spent their best years in the confines of dwindling comfort zones. Our culture indeed wires us for safety and limitations and away from productive decision-making and risk-taking. False security and social approval have become the objects of the natural drive of many individuals. I chose not to be satisfied with the option of tiptoeing through life.

Pain rightly handled can produce both power and peace. Of course, I always had the option of reacting and wallowing in self-pity. I chose instead to put my faith in God and allow Him to direct my path. The archbishop of Uganda, whom I mentioned in a previous chapter, believed and shared a powerful definition of the grace of God: that it is only seen by its effects, that it is an *experience*. Though I did not know that definition early in my life, looking back now I can sense that I was impacted and saturated by that influence of God's presence, His protection, His purpose, and His providence. This very meaningful hymn by an unknown hymn writer, "Show Me Thy Face," certainly undergirded and influenced my spirit, and helped to sustain me.

> Show me Thy face—one transient gleam
> Of loveliness divine,
> And I shall never think or dream
> Of other love save Thine;
>
> Show me Thy face—I shall forget
> The weary days of yore,
> The fretting ghosts of vain regret
> Shall haunt my soul no more;
>
> Show me Thy face—the heaviest cross
> Will then seem light to bear,
> There will be gain in every loss,
> And peace with every care.

The grace of God is only seen by its effects; it is an experience.

The Power of Pushing

Pushes are forces that are able to move something or someone in a direction. For example, it is easy to think of pushing a stalled car. However, people can get stalled as well and remain parked until something or someone pushes them.

Pushing comes from different directions, from different motivations, and from different intentions. While some people are pushed upward, others are pushed aside, pushed around, or pushed down. The push in itself does not make the difference; it is the direction and intention of it that is of paramount significance. Our interpretation of a push, and our reaction and response to it, determines our future. We cannot always control the motivations, the intentions, or the direction of the push, but we can determine where the push takes us and where it lands us. We can feel threatened, terrified, and intimidated by a push, or we can allow God to use the push to fulfill His purpose for our lives.

> *We can feel threatened, terrified, and intimidated by a push, or we can allow God to use the push to fulfill His purpose for our lives.*

Jesus Was Pushed Several Times

I mentioned that Jesus was pushed in several different ways. He was pushed by His mother Mary into performing a miracle, even though at that time He did not believe that His hour had come. He was pushed by the Holy Spirit into the wilderness, to be tempted by Satan.

Public declarations of our faith will always result in great temptations. This is exactly what happened when Jesus was baptized in the Jordan. Matthew 3:16–17 says, "And when Jesus was baptized, immediately he went up from the water, and behold, the heavens were opened to him, and he saw the Spirit of God descending like a dove and coming to rest on him; and behold, a voice from heaven said, 'This is my beloved Son, with whom I am well pleased.'" Right after this tremendous, public, divine affirmation of Jesus, we read in Matthew 4:1, "Then Jesus was led up by the Spirit into the wilderness to be tempted by the devil."

These temptations were indeed pushes and tests that were connected to his mission, and which Hebrews tells us served to accomplish the following three things:

> To destroy the devil's power and free those who were held in slavery by their fear of death (2:14–15).
>
> To position Jesus to become a merciful and faithful High Priest in service to God and atone for our sins (2:17).
>
> To enable Jesus to be the One who is able to sympathize with us in all our weaknesses and infirmities (4:15).

Included among the many hours that Jesus wrestled with Satan in the wilderness (Luke 4:2 tells us that He was tempted by the devil for forty days) was His experience of three specific temptations, which the Gospels tell us about in detail. Jesus' temptations follow three patterns that are common to us all. The first temptation concerns the lust of the flesh:

> Then Jesus was led up by the Spirit into the wilderness to be tempted by the devil. And after fasting forty days and forty nights, he was hungry. And the tempter came and said

to him, "If you are the Son of God, command
these stones to become loaves of bread." But
he answered, "It is written, "'Man shall not live
by bread alone, but by every word that comes
from the mouth of God.'" (Matt. 4:1–4)

Our Lord was hungry, and when the devil tempted Him
to convert stones into bread, but He replied by quoting Deuteronomy 8:3.

The second temptation concerns the pride of
life:
Then the devil took him to the holy city
and set him on the pinnacle of the temple and
said to him, "If you are the Son of God, throw
yourself down, for it is written, "'He will
command his angels concerning you,'
and "On their hands they will bear you up,
lest you strike your foot against a stone.'"
Jesus said to him, "Again it is written, 'You
shall not put the Lord your God to the test.'"
(Matt. 4:5–7)

Notice how Satan's attempt to use scripture specifically (Psalm
91:11–12) to tempt Jesus backfired on him when Jesus himself
rebuked him by quoting Deuteronomy 6:16 ("You shall not put
the Lord your God to the test, as you tested him at Massah.").

Jesus' temptations follow three
patterns that are common to us all.

The third temptation concerns the lust of the eyes.

> Again, the devil took him to a very high
> mountain and showed him all the kingdoms
> of the world and their glory. And he said to
> him, "All these I will give you, if you will fall
> down and worship me." Then Jesus said to
> him, "Be gone, Satan! For it is written, "You
> shall worship the Lord your God and him
> only shall you serve."" (Matt. 4:8–10)

Here we see Satan offering Jesus an alternative, quicker way for Him to complete His mission as Messiah—an option that would have helped Him avoid experiencing the passion and crucifixion for which He had originally come. In the same way, Satan will always offer you and me a shortcut that enables us to avoid paying the price associated with our calling.

In the same way, Satan will always
offer you and me a shortcut that
enables us to avoid paying the price
associated with our calling.

When we are pushed beyond our comfort zone, when we are tempted and tested, let us always remember that Our Lord's human nature enables Him to sympathize with our own weaknesses, because He too was subjected to weakness. He serves as a High Priest who is able to intercede on our behalf and provide the grace of forgiveness, since He too experienced temptations and victories.

May we all find hope and encouragement in knowing that during His time of testing, our Lord was ministered to by angels. During times of testing, pushes and trial, we too are aided by angels who are ministering spirits sent to those who will inherit salvation (Hebrews 1:14).

Wisdom for Living

1. "Everybody gets pushed. How you handle it determines what direction you take and how you push others." How would you explain this to someone?

2. Explain the following statement: "We cannot always control the motivations, the intentions or the direction of the push, but we can determine where the push takes us and where it lands us."

3. Think of and describe an experience in your life that pushed you.

4. God used Joseph's many downward pushes to lift him upward. Explain.

5. In what ways have testings and pushes helped you to become who you are?

Chapter 19

The New Covenant Church of Philadelphia and Campus

O ne of our church's major faith accomplishments was the purchasing of our almost forty-acre historic campus in Philadelphia, Pennsylvania.

The book of James places much emphasis on the importance of demonstrating our faith through our works. It states very clearly that "faith by itself, if it does not have works, is dead" (James 2:17).

Even while I was involved in theological training in Trinidad, West Indies, I started pastoring several churches. My early years in Christian service and ministry helped me to build appropriate relationships with leadership and to contribute to the developing of a practical mission and vision for the church. Following these experiences, I pastored two congregations of the Church of God in the city of George-town in Guyana, South America.

In 1967 I traveled to Philadelphia, Pennsylvania, married my dear wife, and connected with the High Street Church of God, in the Germantown section of the city. Sometime later I was called to became its pastor. After serving faithfully for fifteen years, my wife and I felt the definite call of God to establish the New Covenant Church of Philadelphia. I remember very well the stretching of both obedience and faith my wife and I endured.

Imagine the vision-stretching and risks of faith our board of elders, ministers, deacons, ministry leaders, and almost every member took when, after ten years as a congregation, we prayed, believed God, pursued, and finally purchased the almost forty-acre New Covenant Campus. At the time, we needed to find new facilities for our growing congregation, and yet our finances were very low. In spite of this reality, we had all elevated our level of faith and created a truly skilled, trusted, and capable team of leaders.

The spiritual and physical pilgrimage of the New Covenant Church of Philadelphia began on November 21, 1982, when my wife and I gathered with founding elders the Rev. Abraham and Eve Fenton, Dr. Clarence and Ja'ola Walker, and sixty other worshipers on a cold and rainy night in the chapel at the Manna Bible Institute in Germantown. As the pioneers sat huddled together, warmed only by three kerosene heaters, a prophetic message came forth through the apostle Abraham Fenton from Isaiah 43:19: "Behold, I will do a new thing; now it shall spring forth" (KJV).

The congregation responded with praise and thanksgiving as it sensed that it was being called forth to do great things for God in Philadelphia and beyond.

The Lord continued to bless the new fellowship with "more than it could ask or think"—including a temporary home at

The spiritual and physical pilgrimage of the New Covenant Church of Philadelphia began on November 21, 1982.

Ivy Leaf Middle School on North Broad Street. During this period, I preached a series of sermons on "Partnership with Christ." As I expounded on the new covenant God had made with His church through the sacrifice of Christ, believers began to understand what it meant to be in covenant with God, as Abraham had been. The church grew, and a little over five months later, in April of 1983, the radio ministry *Wisdom from the Word* began.

On the first Sunday in December, 1983, the congregation began worshipping at Messiah Lutheran Church at Broad Street and Roosevelt Boulevard. At that time the membership of the Messiah Lutheran Church had become much smaller and was worshiping on Sunday mornings at 9 a.m. in the church's library. We approached the leadership of the church about renting space for our Sunday services in their sanctuary, which was not being used.

We finally came to an agreement that, instead of their congregation worshiping in their library, they would worship in their sanctuary for an early service, and we could then use the sanctuary for a later service each Sunday. It was indeed a win-win situation.

During that period, many sermons came forth about taking the "risk of faith" and doing great exploits for God. Heeding God's call, the congregation took the risk of faith by making pledges to purchase the former Ramat El Synagogue on Ardleigh Street.

With the purchase of the Ardleigh Street facility, in 1984, New Covenant Church finally had a home of its own. Many gave sacrificially to pay off the thirty-year mortgage in just four years. Services at the Civic Center and Academy of Music highlighted this period. The late 1980s and early 1990s were characterized by tremendous growth, both locally and internationally, in the church's ministries to men, women, youth, and children. On May 18, 1991, I was consecrated as bishop of Covenant Ministries International to better assist the many pastors and ministries from around the world that desire to be under the umbrella of New Covenant.

The purchase of the almost forty-acre former Spring Garden College on May 6, 1993, and the renovation of a number of its major buildings, allowed for the development of ministries such as Covenant International Institute in September 1995. With the completion of a new sanctuary in September 1997, New Covenant Church of Philadelphia is currently striving to prepare for "the latter glory of this house" (Hag. 2:9) as we seek to fulfill our vision of "touching Philadelphia and beyond."

The New Covenant Church campus is situated in the lower Chestnut Hill community of Philadelphia. It has fourteen

With the completion of a new sanctuary in September 1997, New Covenant Church of Philadelphia is currently striving to prepare for "the latter glory of this house" (Hag. 2:9) as we seek to fulfill our vision of "touching Philadelphia and beyond."

buildings, including a gymnasium, several administrative buildings, dormitories, a technical center, a retreat center, and a number of other significant facilities. It is certified as a national historic site by both the State of Pennsylvania and the US Department of Interior. We are significantly grateful for the partnership of Apostle Abraham and Dr. Eve Fenton as well as Dr. and Mrs. Clarence Walker.

God used many people, including the apostles, to write the New Testament. Peter, in Second Peter 1:21, called these writers "holy men of God." We are inspired by and our faith is enlarged by their writings. Now, God through the process of activating our faith to produce works for His kingdom, His glory, and the betterment of humanity, is using us. Actually, God Himself is now personally writing His "brand-New Testament" in the life of each Christian believer. He intends that people will see and read Him through our faith-driven works, for His glory. "You are our epistle written in our hearts, known and read by all men" (2 Cor. 3:2, NKJV).

New Covenant Created a Senior Housing Complex

I have always been committed to ministry to senior citizens. From my teenage years I gave leadership to a team of teenagers who ministered at one or another senior citizens complex every Sunday after the morning service. I remember how, after ministering to the seniors at different institutions, they always said the same thing: "Children, God bless you." It was therefore natural for me, my wife, and a number of our senior leaders to explore the possibility of establishing a complex for senior citizens once we acquired the New Covenant campus.

In the fall of 2004, New Covenant opened an $8.2 million senior housing complex of fifty-six independent apartment units for adults sixty-two years and older who meet income eligibility requirements. These apartments include forty-nine one-bedroom units and seven two-bedroom units that measure 71,132 square feet.

The facility offers supportive services, a seventy-two-seat dining hall, auditorium, transportation, and other amenities designed to help seniors maintain an independent and enjoyable lifestyle.

Faith-Driven Works of God Produce Eternal Benefits

When we allow God to use us, not just through our talk but also through our works, God creates experiences in our lives that literally create in us a consciousness of the supernatural. True faith is unwavering confidence and trust in God's ability and willingness to do the humanly impossible for His children and for His glory. Faith is also a spiritual anchor or consciousness of God's character, which holds us together, and enables us to accomplish God's will for our lives and for

His kingdom, regardless of whatever circumstances break in upon us.

When God uses our faith-driven works, He allows them to become visible testimonies of His leadership and anointing. Every work of faith we pursue is part of a God-directed, perfect preparation, leading us to a future that only God can see.

In John 9:4, Jesus is quoted as saying, "I must work the works of Him that sent Me while it is day: the night is coming when no one can work" (NKJV). As followers of Jesus, we too must commit ourselves to doing the work which God has assigned us with great faith and while we have the time to do it.

True faith is unwavering confidence and trust in God's ability and willingness to do the humanly impossible for His children and for His glory.

Wisdom for Living

1. What does James 2:17 mean when it says that faith without works is dead?
2. What is there in this chapter that reflects the importance of having a working team that shares the same vision?
3. List some benefits we can gain through faith-driven works for God.
4. In what ways is faith a spiritual anchor or consciousness of God's character?

Chapter 20

A Dream of an Assignment
and
Many Vicious Dogs

I n biblical tradition, visions and dreams are an important means God used to communicate with humanity. Of course, not all visions and dreams are from God, but when they are confirmed and fulfilled, one is able to conclude that they are from God.

In the New Testament we read of Peter, Paul, and John having visions. The imagery of John's vision experience is most intriguing and makes up much of the book of Revelation.

My dream was not in the class of the apostles listed above, but it was a revelation from God that continues to have a significant impact on my life.

I had moved from Guyana to Philadelphia, Pennsylvania, in 1967, and got married to my darling wife that year. My first job was with a life insurance company, where I became an effective and honored salesman after being in the business for just six weeks. I was later called to pastor the High Street Church of God in Philadelphia in 1968 and served until 1982.

My Dream and a Transition

My unique dream occurred on the night of January 19, 1994. It was different and unusual. In the dream, I was called to a meeting at a special location. On my arrival I discovered a number of men were there awaiting me. As I entered the room, everyone stood and shook my hand, and I was escorted to a seat at the table. It was clear to me that the meeting had been in progress prior to my arrival and that a decision had been made to call me to attend.

I had a strange feeling. Many questions began rushing through my mind. I remember in my dream wondering what this was all about. Why did they call me, and what would happen to me? At the same time I felt a form of relief when everyone welcomed me by standing and shaking my hand.

The gentleman who seemed to be the chairman began to explain the reason for my invitation. He began by reciting the history of the Church of God in the nation of Guyana in South America. He mentioned the Rev. George Jeffery, the founder of many congregations and a home for the aged in that nation.

The historical presentation ended with a definite surprise as everyone focused singularly on me. The chairman then said, "Dr. Grannum, we invited you here to communicate a decision. You are being appointed to give leadership to what were originally Jeffery's churches and are now the Church of

God in Guyana. We also want you to know that in the process of doing this, you'll be attacked by a number of vicious dogs. Do not be afraid of them. They will bark loudly and attack you. Do not be afraid! *Do not be afraid of them.*"

I remember being stunned and shaken. When I finally woke up, reflected on the dream, and shared it with my wife, I became more stunned and shaken than I had been in my dream.

I then reflected on the instruction Jesus gave in Matthew

> *We also want you to know that in the process of doing this, you'll be attacked by a number of vicious dogs. Do not be afraid of them.*

10:16: "Behold, I am sending you out as sheep in the midst of wolves, so be wise as serpents and innocent as doves." For a minute, I want you to ponder over these two questions:

1. What are the characteristics of wolves?
2. How do they differ from vicious dogs?

Jeffery's Churches

Why were these congregations of the Church of God in Guyana referred to as "Jeffery's churches" in my dream? This reference was to the Rev. George Learmond Jeffrey, the leader of the entire work in British Guiana from its beginning in 1914 until his death in 1949. Following his death, missionaries were sent from Anderson, Indiana, to give leadership to the Church of God in that country.

How Was the January 1994 Dream Fulfilled?

Over time various challenges arose, and the church found itself in crisis. The executive council of the Church of God in Guyana sought the guidance of the regional director, the Rev. Victor Babb, who resided in Barbados. He encouraged the Trinidad zone co-coordinator, Sister Sheila Proctor, to give some assistance to the Guyana church council.

In July of 1994, six months after my dream, Sister Proctor submitted a proposal to the regional director, and in November of 1994 she submitted the same proposal to Guyana's executive council of the Church of God.

On November 16, 1994, ten months after my dream, the regional director of the Caribbean/Atlantic Assembly, the Rev. Victor Babb, wrote to me and asked me to explore the possibility of whatever assistance I could give to my "homeland of Guyana." The regional director stated in his letter to me, "I see no signs of progress in any sphere of the operations of the church in Guyana." He added, "My concern is that if we do nothing, the church will disappear eventually."

On January 6, 1995, one year after my dream, I replied to the regional director that I would travel to Guyana on January 19 to consult directly with the leaders of the Church of God and assess the situation. I arrived in Guyana as promised, met with the executive council and a number of congregational leaders, heard their concerns, and shared in assessing the state of the church. The entire meeting was recorded on tape. I then paid for Sister Sheila Proctor to travel from Trinidad to Barbados to meet with the regional director, the Rev. Victor Babb, and me on March 2. The entire tape of the Guyana meeting was played, and the sentiments of the Guyana church leaders were clearly expressed: the leaders were united in their desire for me to come and serve them in whatever way I could. This request was clearly stated on the tape and heard by the Rev. Babb and Sister Proctor.

> *"My concern is that if we do nothing, the church will disappear eventually."*

After the Barbados meeting, in April, I sent my proposal to both the regional director in Barbados and to the Guyana executive council, based on the request made in Guyana and the clear understanding in Barbados. On June 24, 1995, one year and five months after my dream, the executive council of the Church of God in Guyana passed a unanimous resolution calling my wife, the Rev. Dr. Hyacinth Bobb Grannum, and me to serve the Church of God in Guyana as nonresident missionaries.

This Guyana resolution was also sent to the Caribbean Atlantic Assembly, authorizing our public commissioning and appointment to serve Guyana. This commissioning took place both in Trinidad during the Caribbean Atlantic Association convention and during the Church of God camp meeting in Anderson, Indiana, in June of 1996.

Based on this appointment and commissioning, I was asked to serve as interim chairman for Guyana's general assembly from November 1995 to 1998. Thus the fulfillment of one part of the dream I had in January of 1994. I was not sure of the second part of the dream (about being attacked by vicious dogs, but not to be afraid). At this point, that part of the dream was not yet a reality.

Based on this appointment and commissioning, I was asked to serve as interim chairman for Guyana's general assembly.

The Vicious Dogs Question

In Matthew 10:16–20, Jesus said,

> Behold, I am sending you out as sheep in the midst of wolves, so be wise as serpents and harmless as doves. Beware of men, for they will deliver you over to courts and flog you in their synagogues, and you will be dragged before governors and kings for my sake, to bear witness before them and the Gentiles. When they deliver you over, do not be anxious how you are to speak or what you are to say, for you are to say what will be given to you in that hour. For it is not you who speak, but the Spirit of your Father speaking through you.

Sheep In The Midst Of Wolves

In Matthew 10:5–6, Jesus sends his twelve disciples to minister to a special group of people. "These twelve Jesus sent out, instructing them, 'Go nowhere among the Gentiles, and enter no town of the Samaritans, but go rather to the lost sheep of the house of Israel.'" He continues in Matthew 10:16,

"Behold, I am sending you out as sheep in the midst of wolves, so be wise as serpents and innocent as doves."

Isn't that fascinating? Jesus is sending His disciples to minister to the lost house of Israel, and He is referring to them as wolves in terms of their possible response to the gospel message and to Him as the Messiah. Why "wolves"?

Wolves, like people, have personalities, and no two wolves are alike. Personalities develop through one's individual unique emotions, experiences and thoughts, which result in different actions, reactions and behaviors. By nature, wolves are social and respond in a friendly and communal way towards other wolves and their pups. The strongest quality of wolves seems to be the capacity to quickly and firmly connect with, make emotional attachment with, and socialize with other wolves. Wolves feel a sense of group security and are protective of their own kind. The reason they are seen as savage, vicious, and aggressive is because they respond negatively to any outside interference or seeming penetration.[21]

Among followers of Judaism, Jesus was viewed as having been the most effective and influential leader, and therefore the most damaging, of all the persons claiming to be the Messiah. It was their understanding that when the true Messiah came, he would overthrow the Romans and establish a kingdom of which they would be in charge.

Is it possible that some established leaders in Guyana felt threatened by my wife and me having been appointed to give leadership to the church in that country?

Jesus' admonition to the disciples to be wise as serpents represents the wisdom, carefulness and cautiousness necessary in ministering and presenting Him as the Messiah to this religiously closed group.

Imagine a flock of helpless sheep in the midst of a pack of protective wolves that feel threatened. Is it possible that some established leaders in Guyana felt threatened by my wife and me having been appointed to give leadership to the church in that country?

A Vicious Court Case in 1999

In 1999 a court case was launched by number of individuals against my wife and me. It was encouraged by a number of leaders from the Caribbean and two pastors within the Church of God in Guyana. The purpose of the court action was to prevent us from serving the church in Guyana. On the first day of the court hearing, the lawyer of the many plaintiffs stood and in a painstaking way stated their case against my wife, me, and our leadership. The next speaker was our attorney, the Rev. James A. Patterson, a retired judge.

I had encouraged him to focus on the major principle of the Church of God, and that was "The Principle of Autonomy." This principle, also understood as "self-rule," holds that every entity of the Church of God has the authority to select its own leadership. No outside person or system can override this principle of governance. Each congregation has "self-rule." And this applies to all general or national bodies of the Church of God in Guyana.

"Since the Bishop and his wife were officially and unanimously called and commissioned by the appropriate national body of the Church of God in Guyana," our attorney said, "and since that commissioning was repeated in both Barbados and Anderson, Indiana, therefore there can be no basis for a legal case against them."

After carefully listening to both attorneys, the judge made an absolutely unusual statement. "Brothers and sisters, after listening to both sides, I am convinced that there is nothing expressed here that could not be settled in a simple one-hour prayer meeting." Before the judge could continue, one of the plaintiffs, a pastor, jumped up and shouted, "Judge, let's leave prayer out of this!"

The judge was stunned and astonished. He looked at the pastor in amazement. Immediately he realized that he was dealing with a contrary spirit. After a long pause, he postponed the case, and it has not been called up to the date of this writing. When—and if—the case is finally resumed, we will have to inform the judge that all the plaintiffs and accusers, those from within the country and those outside of it, as well as their attorney, have since died.

"Judge, let's leave prayer out of this!"

As I reflect on how I was both informed and warned by my dream in 1994, I cannot help but be reminded of God's words in Joshua 1:9: "Have I not commanded you? Be strong and courageous. Do not be frightened, and do not be dismayed, for the LORD your God is with you wherever you go."

Wisdom for Living

1. What do you think of the fact that so many aspects of my dream actually came to pass within a short space of time?
2. How do you think God used the dream to help prepare me for experiences that would come to my life?
3. What insights have you gained in relation to understanding the principle of divine timing?
4. How do you assess the wisdom and discernment of a judge who after listing to both sides said, "Brothers and sisters, after listening to both sides, I am convinced that there is nothing expressed here that could not be settled in a simple one-hour prayer meeting?"
5. What is your assessment of the pastor who interrupted the judge and shouting, "Judge, let's leave prayer out of this!"

Chapter 21

Self-Made Giants
in Your Path

Having a purpose in life and a clear vision will always put you at risk and position you to be surrounded by self-made giants.

Self-made giants refer to individuals or groups of persons, organizations, institutions, attitudes, mindsets, or perceptions that you allow to impact the way you see yourself and the decisions you make. They make it difficult or cause you not to be able to view yourself the way God made you and sees you.

There are two types of self-made giants. The first set convinces themselves that they are stronger, bigger, better, and more knowledgeable than you or anyone else around them.

The second set of self-made giants are the ones we ourselves create out of fear, uncertainty, and lack of faith in God.

We feel we need to look continuously for someone else's approval, then we make those individuals giants in our lives. Later, we are surprised how both of these self-made giants position themselves in our path to hinder and block us at almost every turn.

The unique thing about self-made giants is that they tend to take themselves seriously and expect you to do the same. Actually, a close examination of self-made giants will definitely remind you of author Hans Christian Andersen's tale of "The Emperor's New Clothes."[22] Two weavers had promised the Emperor a new suit of clothes that was invisible to those who were unfit for their positions, stupid, or incompetent. When the Emperor paraded before his subjects in his "new clothes," no one dared to say that they don't see any suit of clothes until a child cried out, "But he isn't wearing anything at all!" That tale has been translated into over one hundred languages.

Imagine the shock that comes to self-made giants when they realize that you see both their nakedness and their needs. Think of the dismay they feel when they know that you see them differently, and you will therefore not give in their demands and expectations.

When we don't understand who we are and our God-given assignment, we usually feel the need to take naked, self-made giants seriously.

Over the decades, every undertaking my wife and I have pursued came with giants—demonic giants—whose strategies were to distract us, disturb us, degrade us, defeat us, and destroy us at every turn. Jesus made this reality of conflict with giants very clear. He said the thief comes "only to steal and kill and destroy" (John 10:10). Giants are actively seeking to kill our hopes, our dreams, our faith, our vision and our possibilities. Giants come to disrupt our present and to disturb and prevent our future.

> *Giants come to disrupt our present and to disturb and prevent our future.*

Your Land Of Canaan Comes With Giants

In the book of Numbers 13:1–2, God's people under the leadership of Moses and Aaron reached close the land God had promised them, and were instructed to search it out for 40 days. Here is how the Bible puts it: "The Lord spoke to Moses, saying, 'Send some men to spy out the land of Canaan, which I am giving to the people of Israel. From each tribe of their fathers you shall send a man, everyone a chief among them.'" In Numbers 13:31–33, they returned to God with their assessment and report.

Read the two different reports carefully.

In Numbers 13:30, following a general report regarding the resources of the land, the topography, the structure of the cities and the physiology of the people who inhabited the land Moses and Aaron received a specific report from Caleb who encouraged the people by saying, "Let us go up at once and occupy it, for we are well able to overcome it."

In verses 31–33 a second report is given as follows:

> Then the men who had gone up with him said, "We are not able to go up against the people, for they are stronger than we are."

> So they brought to the people of Israel a bad
> report of the land that they had spied out,
> saying, "The land, through which we have
> gone to spy it out, is a land that devours its
> inhabitants, and all the people that we saw in
> it are of great height. And there we saw the
> Nephilim (the sons of Anak, who come from
> the Nephilim), and we seemed to ourselves
> like grasshoppers, and so we seemed to them.

This second report given by the majority of the spies who had gone up with Caleb reveals two major perception problems:

1. Their perception of the inhabitants of the land that God was giving them.
2. Their perception of themselves as the people of God and what He was giving them as a possession.

The first problem deals with the people's perception of the inhabitants of the land. They saw them as giants. In other words, what they described to the others was not reality, but rather a figment of their imagination, and thus, they were self-made giants. Consequently, the Israelites thought to themselves:

- We can't attack those people.
- They are stronger than we are.
- The land devours those living in it.
- All the people we saw there are like giants.

What they described to the others
was not reality, but rather a figment
of their imagination, and thus,
they were self-made giants.

The second problem had to do with their perception of themselves as the people of God and what He was giving them as a possession. In their estimation:

- All the people the spies saw were like giants to them.
- In light of the first observation, they saw themselves as grasshoppers.
- They assumed that the inhabitants of the land saw them, too, as grasshoppers.

Facts Versus Realities

The twelve leaders sent to scout out the land all saw the same facts, but not the same realities. In the case of the ten spies, their facts created panic. In the case of Caleb and Joshua, their trust in God created a reality that gave them confidence and peace. What made the difference? It was in this. The ten spies compared themselves with the giants, while Caleb and Joshua compared the giants with God. This is what they said to the people: "The LORD is with us; do not fear them" (Numbers 14:9).

Faith always looks beyond the challenges of the difficulties to the greatness of the opportunities under God. The wall is always too solid and high for me, but with my faith and God's touch, it will fall down like cardboard. Giants stand for great difficulties and are stalking us everywhere. They are in our families, in our churches, in our social life, and in our politics and have positioned themselves even in our hearts and minds. Unless we live conscious of them, we cannot begin the process of overcoming them. What we do not seek and struggle to overcome could eventually overwhelm us and destroy us.

Now the fact is, unless we have the overcoming faith, we shall be eaten up and consumed by the giants in our path. Let us have the spirit of faith that Moses and Aaron, of Caleb and Joshua. See God and focus on Him, and He will take care of the difficulties. It is when we are pursuing our mission and in the way of duty, so to speak, that we find giants. It was when Israel was moving toward and very close to what God had promised them that these imaginary, self-made giants appeared.

There is a prevalent idea that the power of God in a human life should lift us above all trials and conflicts. The truth is that the power of God always brings a conflict and a struggle. This was true in Jesus' life and that of the apostles and leaders of the Christian faith. One would have thought that on his great missionary journey to Rome, Paul would have been carried by some mighty providence above the power of storms and tempests and enemies. On the contrary, his journey was one long, hard-fought battle persecuting Jews, with venomous vipers and all the powers of earth and hell. Then at last he was saved by swimming ashore at Malta on a piece of wreckage and barely escaping a watery grave.[23]

Does this account illustrate God as one who has infinite power? You may say no, but it actually does. Paul tells us that when he took the Lord Jesus Christ as the life of his body, a severe conflict immediately came; indeed, a conflict that never ended, a pressure that was persistent, but out of which he always emerged victorious through the strength of Jesus Christ. No matter the circumstances, the shipwrecks (giants) that you face, like Paul you could face them with the courage that comes from the assurance that you will always emerge victorious.

This is what he says in Second Corinthians 4:8–11 (KJV):

> We are troubled on every side, yet not
> distressed; we are perplexed, but not in
> despair; Persecuted, but not forsaken; cast
> down, but not destroyed; Always bearing
> about in the body the dying of the Lord Jesus,
> that the life also of Jesus might be made
> manifest in our body. For we which live are
> always delivered unto death for Jesus' sake,
> that the life also of Jesus might be made
> manifest in our mortal flesh.

When we misunderstand or have confusion about who we are, our assignment, and who it is that assigned it to us, we always end up focusing on a false reality of giants. We will always find ourselves focusing on self-made giants when our faith is not significantly grounded in the person, promises, and power of God. Whenever we seek to pursue anything of significance in our own strength, our humanness automatically creates obstacles—self-made giants—that either to hinder us or seek to claim the glory.

True faith in God gives God the upper hand, but limited faith gives self-made giants the upper hand. It was D.L. Moody who said, "Trust in yourself and you are doomed to disappointment. Trust in your friends, and they will leave you. Trust in money, and you may have it taken from you. But trust in God, and you are never to be confounded in time or eternity."

Do you want a fearless faith? Be careful not to measure or compare the images or strength of the real giants, as well as the perceived giants with your strength in God. Remember that God is working for you to will and do of His own good pleasure (Philippians 2:13). If He is for you, who can be against you? (Rom. 8:31).

"And we seemed to ourselves like *grasshoppers*, and so we seemed to them" (Numbers 13:33). Change your thinking and your view of yourself. Remind yourself that you and I are sons and daughters of the living God, and that we "can do all things through Him who strengthens us" (Philippians 4:13).

Wisdom for Living

1. How would you explain to a child the meaning of the story of "The Emperor's New Clothes"?
2. How do people face giants when they see themselves as grasshoppers?
3. Why do some tend to go through life seeing themselves as grasshoppers?
4. How would you describe a grasshopper mentality?
5. How did God use Paul's faith and mindset to bring about his deliverances?

Chapter 22

Don't Judge God
Too Early

My wife and I were on a cruise some time ago. One morning as we sat to have breakfast in the dining room, another passenger made a very interesting request of me. "Could you share something of your life journey?"

As I told him about my life, I realized that so many of our blessings came from and through God and His working through three vehicles in our lives and the lives of our family.

1. The vehicle of the many early dreams and vision that filled our minds and spirits.
2. The many positive and encouraging people God allowed to surface in our lives.

3. The works and intentions of those who chose to be our enemies.

Handling all three of these well gives God an opportunity to prove that what is meant for evil can definitely be made to work towards our good. Based on this fact and all the divine operations that create these realities, we could surely put our absolute trust in God.

Later on that week, I was reflecting on an idea. It must be somewhat difficult to trust a God who has never been tried. My wife and I grew up being taught to love God with our hearts, minds, souls, and strength. This concept was in many of the hymns and songs we learned in church, Sunday school and then vacation Bible school. We had a reasonably good grasp of what it means to love God and love our parents. We understood that this level of loving God was much higher than how we should seek to really like our friends or even other people.

Yet we have to ask the question, can one truly love a God whom he or she has never put to the test? The Bible gives us many powerful insights on how to answer this question, but a very practical and powerful one is in Malachi 3:10 (ESV): "Bring the full tithe into the storehouse, that there may be food in my house. And thereby put me to the test, says the LORD of hosts, if I will not open the windows of heaven for you and pour down for you a blessing until there is no more need."

I honestly believe that my wife's and my deepest insights about God came from the ways we have been forced to test Him, then to trust Him. From our early years, as we were introduced to Jesus, we made the decisions to give Him our hearts and to trust Him with our lives.

We see this principle very clearly as we study the journey of Joseph and how the experiences of his journey forced him to trust God and eventually pushed him into greatness.

His story is found in the book of Genesis starting at chapter 37. He lived in Canaan and was the son of Jacob. Since

I honestly believe that my wife's and my deepest insights about God came from the ways we have been forced to test Him, then to trust Him.

he was Jacob's youngest son and was born in his father's old age, his father loved him dearly and made him a special coat of many colors. This caused his brothers to be very envious of him and to actually hate him. In addition, Joseph at age seventeen began to dream big dreams that caused his brothers to hate him even more.

One day, while his brothers were taking care of their father's sheep in the fields, they saw him from afar, and before he came near to them they conspired against him to kill him, "They said to one another, 'Here comes this dreamer. Come now, let us kill him and throw him into one of the pits. Then we will say that a fierce animal has devoured him, and we will see what will become of his dreams'" (Gen. 37:18–20). Reuben, his older brother, suggested that rather than killing him, that he be sold for twenty shekels of silver to a group of Ishmaelites who were on their way to Egypt. Later, in Egypt, he was sold to Potiphar, an officer of Pharaoh and captain of the guard.

In Egypt, as part of Pharaoh's household, Joseph became a leader without his brothers and members of his family back in Canaan knowing it. They had helped to literally push him to greatness without knowing or intending it. They could never have imagined that what they were doing to him with an evil intent was being used by God to accomplish His supernatural purposes, not just for Joseph or for his family, but for the world.

Many years later, Joseph's brothers, with fear and trembling, discovered him in his royally appointed position and with national influence in Egypt. Joseph, on discovering them, calmed their fears with a powerful statement found in Genesis 50:19–21:

They could never have imagined that what they were doing to him with an evil intent was being used by God to accomplish His supernatural purposes.

But Joseph said to them, "Do not fear, for am I in the place of God? As for you, you meant evil against me, but God meant it for good, to bring it about that many people should be kept alive, as they are today. So do not fear; I will provide for you and your little ones." Thus he comforted them and spoke kindly to them.

God had enabled Joseph to turn his bitter water into wine of which there was an abundance. Joseph discovered that there is no fulfilling destiny without sacrifice.

The story of Joseph speaks to the way the Christian life works most of the time. It requires sacrifices yet offering the assurance that when you are doing God's business, He is working with and for you. Many times it is hard to tell what God is actually doing on our behalf because we are simply looking around at the challenging circumstances that confront us. We spend many of our days simply wishing that God would clarify His works and His purposes towards us. How challenging it is for us during these times to trust that God is working everything out for our good based on His promises. For a long period of time, this was the mental and psychological valley of pain and perplexity in which Joseph found himself living on a daily basis.

In Genesis 37:5–8, 26–28, and 50:15–21, we see Joseph emerging from the painful valley, and with God's help we discern the significant insights of wisdom, perspective, and power by asking these and other questions.

- What can we learn from Joseph and how God manifested Himself on Joseph's behalf?
- What do you think Joseph's mindset became when he discovered that based on God's plan for his life he would one day rule over his brothers?
- How do you think his brothers felt when they finally realized that Joseph was now ruler over them?

In fullness of time, his brothers realized that his dream for which they hated him had actually come to pass. Interestingly, their very betrayal of Joseph caused him to be taken to Egypt, which ended up being part of God's directly manifested purpose for his life and for the survival of his brethren. At the end of Genesis, after Jacob's death, Joseph's brothers begged him to forgive them of their transgressions against him.

In Genesis 50:19–21, when they spoke to him, he said to them, "Do not fear, for am I in the place of God? As for you, you meant evil against me, but God meant it for good, to bring it about that many people should be kept alive, as they are today. So do not fear; I will provide for you and your little ones."

The hurt his brothers' betrayal caused him was real. The evil they had done to him was grievous and life impacting. Yet, one cannot help but notice that Joseph, one of the most powerful men in Egypt, refused to take the path of revenge or retaliation. He saw a greater plan at work that led him to forgive them and seek their good. He understood the awesome power of forgiveness and demonstrated it even to their surprise.

He also understood the significant difference between forgiveness and pardon. You may forgive one who wronged you and still continue to hope for a just punishment of the person

Yet, one cannot help but notice that Joseph, one of the most powerful men in Egypt, refused to take the path of revenge or retaliation.

for that wrong. What most of us often fail to understand is that the only thing harder than forgiveness is the challenge of having to live day by day with the alternative. Joseph knew that true forgiveness has the potential of transformation in the guilty party. It's a type of spiritual surgery whereby you intentionally slice away the wrong from the person who did it to you and begin to see that person as a new and different individual. Forgiveness allows you to actually remake the person in your memory.

But Joseph understood a greater and far more significant spiritual principle. One of the greatest evidences of true faith and trust in God is that we must refuse to harbor bitterness and anger toward others during a conflict. If we truly believe that God is working everything out and doing it every day on our behalf, then we have to trust Him and focus on Him and not on our enemies. When we take the time to really study God's wise providence, we will conclude every time, like Joseph, "You meant evil against me; but God meant it for good" (Gen. 50:20).

It is important to note that while both the Lord and our enemies may use the same things to influence us, God uses them for a different and higher purpose.

Look at how Jesus confirmed and affirmed the spirit in which Joseph responded to his circumstances. The Bible says of Jesus, "When he was reviled, He did not revile in return; when He suffered, He did not threaten, but continued entrusting himself to Him who judges justly. He himself bore our sins in his body on the tree, that we might die to sin and live to righteousness" (1 Peter 2:23–24). We too must constantly entrust ourselves to the one who judges justly; it is not our place to judge others' actions. When we do, we demonstrate how disconnected we are from the One who works out all things for our good.

As I have reflected on Joseph's life and the questions posed in this section, I believe that if Joseph could shout a message to us from the house top, it would be, "Don't judge God too early." When you find yourself in dire circumstances, when life dishes out the unexpected, when those you love most, trusted the most betray you, when all seems lost, I say to you, *don't judge God too early*. He is working for you and through you, even in the valley.

> ## *He is working for you and through you, even in the valley.*

God's School of Preparation

Moses was in God's school of preparation, not for days, weeks, or months, but for eighty years—forty years in the house of Pharaoh and forty years in the wilderness before his work of leading Israel began. He was 120 years old when he finally saw his life's work fulfilled. He went through a very thorough and lengthy leadership development process.

His Old Testament contemporaries also experienced extended developmental processes. Abraham waited twenty-five years for a promised son. It took Noah 120 years to build the ark to protect the righteous during the flood. Joseph was imprisoned for fourteen years for a crime he didn't commit, and Job waited for what is a lifetime for some, sixty to seventy years, for God's justice.

Waiting on God deepens and matures us, widens our perspective, and broadens our understanding while we are enduring seasons that are seemingly unfruitful. When, we navigate in the right perspective, these seasons help us recognize and seize the opportunities that exist but are not easily discernible.

When you succeed in not judging God too early, you will make one of the most significant discoveries of life. God is involved in absolutely everything! William Cowper was born in 1731 in Berkhamsted, England. His mother died when he was only six years old, leaving him to be raised by his father. Unfortunately, it seems that he had an unhealthy relationship with his father, who pushed him into studying law early in his life.

In much of his life, he struggled with ongoing depression. He had four major battles with it, leading him to attempt suicide on several occasions. However, God preserved his life each time.

In 1764, while a patient at St. Albans Insane Asylum, he found a Bible on a bench in the garden, and God used John 11 and Romans 3:25 to open his eyes to the goodness of Jesus, the sufficiency of his atoning work, and the sovereignty and goodness of God.

He became attracted to the work of John Newton who had written the hymn "Amazing Grace." This association began to bring out Cowper's poetic skills, and John Newton began to mentor him in the developing of this definite gift. They took long walks and spent much time together discussing the Scriptures and pondering the purposes of God for their lives, for the world, and for His church.

Cowper's hymnwriting came as a result of his friendship with John Newton. They became friends in 1767 when Cowper moved to Olney, England, to be under Newton's ministry.

Newton saw Cowper's bent to melancholy and reclusiveness and drew him into the ministry of visitation as much as he could. While walking between parishioners' homes, they would talk of God and his purposes for the church.

In 1769 Newton got the idea of collaborating with Cowper on a book of hymns to be sung by their church and through music to instruct believers in the principles and teachings of their Christian faith. In the end Newton wrote about 208 hymns and Cowper wrote 68. The hymnal was published in 1779. Besides "Amazing Grace," Newton wrote "How Sweet the Name of Jesus Sounds," "Glorious Things of Thee Are Spoken," and "Come, My Soul Thy Suit Prepare." Among the hymns Cowper wrote were "There is a Fountain Filled with Blood," "O For a Closer Walk with God," and "God Moves in a Mysterious Way."

The hymn "God Moves in a Mysterious Way" is a combination of assertions intending to teach believers about God's goodness, sovereignty, and wisdom and the importance of developing courage and truly trusting God in every situation. The hymn is a beautiful expression of the kind of faith that sustained Cowper through long periods of mental illness, darkness and despair.

This phrase, "God moves in a mysterious way," reflects deep, divine revelation. It became a popular saying for moments when answers were sought and could not be found. When answers seem to elude you, when you have come to the end of yourself, may the message and the words of this hymn offer you the same reassurance they have offered to believers over the centuries:

> God moves in a mysterious way
> His wonders to perform;
> He plants his footsteps in the sea,
> And rides upon the storm.
>
> Deep in unfathomable mines
> of never-failing skill
> He treasures up his bright designs,
> and works His sov'reign will.
>
> Ye fearful Saints, fresh courage take;
> The clouds ye so much dread
> Are big with mercy and shall break
> In blessings on your head.
>
> His purposes will ripen fast,
> Unfolding every hour;
> The bud may have a bitter taste,
> But sweet will be the flower.
> Blind unbelief is sure to err,
> And scan his works in vain;
> God is his own interpreter,
> And he will make it plain.[24]

This phrase, "God moves in a mysterious way," reflects deep, divine revelation.

Wisdom for Living

1. When you look back at your journey how do you understand the thought, "Don't judge God too early"?
2. As Joseph reflected on his life and the role of his brothers, he remarked, "You meant evil against me; but God meant it for good." How does this statement relate to your journey?
3. Reflect on, and discuss the following: The only thing harder than forgiveness is the challenge of having to live day by day with the alternative.
4. Explain the following: "Forgiveness is a type of spiritual surgery whereby you intentionally slice away the wrong from the person who did it to you, and begin to see that person as a new and different individual. Forgiveness allows you to actually remake the person in your memory."
5. How would you explain this verse of the great hymn?

> Blind unbelief is sure to err,
>   And scan his works in vain;
> God is his own interpreter,
>   And he will make it plain.

Chapter 23

Dare to Pursue
the Difficult

I have already mentioned in this book the tremendous experiences my friend Dr. Ernest Wilson and I had as we were ministering to thousands of persons in Uganda, East Africa. The services lasted for several days, and there were thousands of individuals present every day and for many of the night services. Something different was happening in addition to the Scripture being taught. Several times there would be a breakout of celebration and of thanksgiving because special things were happening during the session.

We actually experienced signs and wonders taking place regularly during those sessions that week. As we were singing, praying, and teaching, there would be in certain places a breakout in celebration, because right there in that service, at that moment, somebody was being healed. It was indeed a touching and new experience for those in attendance who were from the United States and England.

Looking back now and trying to capture the whole environment and the powerful manifestations of the Spirit of God that we all experienced in those meetings, we feel that all of that contributed to president Idi Amin's attempt to capture Dr. Wilson and me and later to kill the Archbishop.

The truth is that we and other visitors from outside of East Africa did not bring the revival or contribute much to the burst of spiritual energy we all experienced there. It was almost like God desiring to do something and taking advantage of this opportunity where there was an expectation to receive.

True faith is actually desiring and choosing to believe and to do something different. In that respect, faith always requires risk. We cannot trust God and prove Him without taking the risks and testing required.

Sometimes when you seek to move forward, stretch forth, and follow Christ's demands, you will think you are stepping out into a void, but that void will turn to rock beneath your feet. Remember, the whole earth was without form and void until God spoke the word. Many of these individuals in the services in Uganda came with faith to experience something different, and our God, our faith-seeing and faith-honoring God, responded.

We cannot trust God and prove Him without taking the risks and testing required.

Your "little faith" starts a process that puts your life and God on a cooperative path. Faith seals the partnership and manages the plan. The following is a very powerful example of how that works:

> He went on from there and entered their
> synagogue. And a man was there with a
> withered hand. And they asked him, "Is it
> lawful to heal on the Sabbath?"— so that they
> might accuse him. He said to them, "Which
> one of you who has a sheep, if it falls into a pit
> on the Sabbath, will not take hold of it and
> lift it out? Of how much more value is a man
> than a sheep! So it is lawful to do good on the
> Sabbath." Then he said to the man, "Stretch
> out your hand." And the man stretched it out,
> and it was restored, healthy like the other. But
> the Pharisees went out and conspired against
> him, how to destroy him. (Matt. 12:9–14)

Four major realities are at work in this passage:

1. Jesus enters the synagogue where He was always under suspicion and with a risk of being falsely judged.
2. There was a sick man there with a definite need and with possible faith to be healed.
3. God had an opportunity to do something quite different and receive the glory.
4. The Pharisees present expected Jesus to do something that was different and contrary to the traditions of

their synagogue, yet consistent with His anointing and passion.

With all this in play, the religious leaders saw their golden opportunity to confront Jesus in order to accomplish their objectives. It was a perfect setup.

Luke 6:7 states, "And the scribes and the Pharisees watched him, to see whether he would heal on the Sabbath, so that they might find a reason to accuse him." Jesus decided to pursue the difficult. He always worked and ministered under the malignant eye of the orthodox leaders.

They followed Him like private detectives, seeking evidence on which to level charges against Him. They knew He would heal the sick, but to heal the sick on the Sabbath would be in violation of religious tradition, and would enable them to accuse Him of healing by the power of the devil. Jesus looked at the man with pity and compassion. The leaders noticed the man looking at Jesus with desperate hope of being touched and healed. The scribes and Pharisees' moment had come.

Jesus decided to pursue the difficult.

They confronted Jesus with the religious question that revealed their real motives and through which they might accuse Him. "Is it lawful to heal on the Sabbath?" Jesus answered the leaders with the parable recorded in Matthew 12:11–12: "He said to them, 'Which one of you who has a sheep, if it falls into a pit on the Sabbath, will not take hold of it and lift it out? Of how much more value is a man than a sheep! So it is lawful to do good on the Sabbath.'" Having said that, Jesus went on to focus on the man's needs. "Then he said to the man, 'Stretch out your hand'" (v. 13).

Stretching out his hand was the one thing he couldn't do and probably had not done in decades. The command went through his ears, probably to his heart, impacted his mind, and was processed by his spirit before he could probably capture the reality and implications of Jesus' words, "Stretch out your hand."

See the realization in his eyes and the energy he exerts to lift up his arm and to stretch it forth. What we cannot see was the internal effort of mixing his little grain of faith with his will to pursue the difficult and push in the direction of his miracle. Imagine the helpless astonishment with which this man looked at Jesus. He began to raise that arm, and lo, in the very process of obedience, the strength came and the miracle was manifested. His hand "was restored, healthy like the other."

He began to raise that arm, and lo, in the very process of obedience, the strength came and the miracle was manifested.

This incident became a crucial moment in this man's life as well as in the life of Jesus. In this act, Jesus deliberately and publicly broke the Sabbath tradition. Matthew 12:14 records the consequences of this act: "But the Pharisees went out and conspired against him, how to destroy him."

It is reported that when communism began to die in parts of Eastern Europe, many older Eastern Europeans who knew nothing but the communist system began to experience a sense of loss. The question some of them began to ask themselves was, "What are we going to do?"

The old economic system was quickly crumbling, and the new order was about to emerge. The key to balance and stability for these individuals was to help them take little steps in the new direction. It took a big effort to muster up even a little faith in the newly emerging system of capitalism. Those little steps of faith came as people were helped to answer another question: "What do you want for your future?" The want of a better life was the starting point for the new risks that were needed. This process began a type of conversion that that little faith began to produce.

This same conversion process holds true for our faith in Jesus Christ. At a time when many churches are allowing the concept of conversion to slip into the background, psychologists and psychiatrists are reemphasizing its importance. They are not using the same language or the same belief in God, but they are telling us that our innermost beings are calling for more than things and pleasures and that effective and creative living requires moral considerations and spiritual underpinning. They state that these moral and spiritual underpinnings help people to capture a sense of purpose for their lives.

God puts within us moral considerations and spiritual underpinnings that are connected to true conversion. Conversion through Christ is a spiritual process through which God unifies the personality and brings harmony into the center of life. Jesus stated a truly difficult truth: "Unless one is born again he cannot see the kingdom of God" (John 3:3).

What did He mean by being "born again"? To be born again is to be born from above. Our natural life, which is from

Conversion through Christ is a spiritual process through which God unifies the personality and brings harmony into the center of life.

below, is driven by instincts that reside in the unconscious and literally control the conscious mind, resulting in all of the lusts of our lower nature.

The Christian gospel is good news that produces a new self in persons who believe and embrace it. In the quietness of your heart, you must make that difficult choice between the lower and the higher life, between life from below and life from above.

In Matthew 12:43–46, Jesus told of a house that was swept and furnished, yet left empty. Our modern technological society has swept away many foundational beliefs and left us with lives full of new electronic toys for adults, yet empty of a working faith for constructive living. A friend of mine from another country visited my office a while ago. He shared his passion and his vision to minister to individuals in his home country. He added, "My heart was broken one day when I arrived at a house and was amazed to find an infant tugging at the breast of a lifeless mother." Easy living is life without Christ—a life of emptiness that makes human beings like that motherless, hungry infant.

Jesus answers the question of our emptiness by sharing with us some more very difficult truth:

> I am the way, and the truth, and the life. No one comes to the Father except through me. (John 14:6)

> The thief comes only to steal and kill and destroy. I came that they may have life and have it abundantly. (John 10:10)
>
> Come to me, all who labor and are heavy laden, and I will give you rest. Take my yoke upon you, and learn from me, for I am gentle and lowly in heart, and you will find rest for your souls. For my yoke is easy, and my burden is light. (Matt. 11:28–30)

He alone can fill our emptiness and give us both purpose and peace that is beyond human understanding. That one step of faith may seem difficult in your mind. Go ahead and make the difficult decision. It will begin the most powerful and life-changing process you could ever experience. Always dare to pursue the difficult.

> *He alone can fill our emptiness and give us both purpose and peace that is beyond human understanding.*

Wisdom for Living

1. What three major realities were at work in the Matthew 12:9–14 story?
2. How do you deal with situations where you know that you are surrounded by enemies?

3. In Matthew 12: 11–12, where was Jesus' real focus, on the possible reaction of the enemies or on the healing of the sick man? Explain your answer.

4. How did Jesus' pursuit of the difficult bring healing to the sick man and glory to God?

5. Why do most people find it so much easier to back away rather than pursuing the difficult?

Chapter 24

True Faith Has Power for Your Possibilities

In his promises, God shows us his storehouse of abounding provision. Faith is the key that opens the storehouse. And God wants us to open his storehouse!

—Jon Bloom

I am always intrigued by verses in the Bible that begin with the following: "By faith Abraham . . ."! "By faith Moses . . ."! "By faith Joshua . . ."! "By faith Rehab . . ."! How can our lives reflect "By faith you . . ." or "By faith I . . ."?

Over the years, I believe the Lord has been seeking to train me and make me conscious of the reality that everything I really need can come through Him by faith in Him. It is almost as if He expands my life based on my own faith, and I participate in narrowing my life by my lack of faith.

Looking back, when I was made homeless at age fourteen, I experienced much mental and emotional pain, but no panic. I was put out, but I never felt lost or abandoned. I felt confident that God was in the picture, and somewhere or somehow He would provide for me. As a teenager, I was pouring my time, my energy, my talent, and my life into serving Him and helping to build His kingdom, and I was confident in my faith and in the theological truth behind one of the hymns we sang at church:

> Be not dismayed whate'er betide,
> God will take care of you!
> Beneath His wings of love abide,
> God will take care of you!
>
> God will take care of you,
> Through every day o'er all the way;
> He will take care of you;
> God will take care of you!
>
> Through days of toil when heart doth fail,
> God will take care of you!
> When dangers fierce your path assail,
> God will take care of you!

> All you may need He will provide,
> God will take care of you!
> Trust Him, and you will be satisfied,
> God will take care of you!
>
> No matter what may be the test,
> God will take care of you!
> Lean, weary one, upon His breast,
> God will take care of you!

Hebrews 11:6 speaks of the importance of faith. "And without faith it is impossible to please him, for whoever would draw near to God must believe that he exists and that he rewards those who seek him." This verse clearly indicates that the path to pleasing God is through faith. It also suggests that the path to the success of any undertaking is through faith. Faith is not simply a religious concept. It empowers every person who truly understands it. If it were simply a religious concept, Jesus would not instruct us in Mark 11:22 to "have faith in God." In other words, regardless of one's religious persuasion, one who has faith in God is positioned to experience Him and His power.

This verse clearly indicates that the path to pleasing God is through faith.

The absolute power of faith in God confirms that we shall have whatever we truly pursue. There is an almost unlimited potential to faith that is grounded in God. Its creative power is contained within itself and generates fruits according to its kind.

Mary was bold in her undertaking based on her faith in Jesus. When the need arose, she did not call a committee of persons of unlike faith. Even Jesus' disciples who were with Him had not yet believed in Him. Had she consulted with the servants who brought the news of the shortage of wine, she would have been fettered by their past experiences.

Intellectual belief is not faith. Just to say you believe is not the same as having faith. You and I are trained to believe many things about which we have no real intelligent faith. Biblical faith has to do solely with what is written in the Word of God, the promises He has made, and the nature of His character. Intelligent faith goes far beyond our feelings and that which is logical and reasonable. It says, "If I really believe the promises of God, then all things are possible."

Through the prophet Isaiah, God made some promises about Jesus: "And the Spirit of the Lord shall rest upon him, the Spirit of wisdom and understanding, the Spirit of counsel and might, the Spirit of knowledge and the fear of the LORD" (Isaiah 11:2).

Do you think Jesus' knowledge of the prophecies influenced the life He lived and the miracles He performed? I believe that it did and that He lived conscious of His anointing. How would a consciousness of our anointing strengthen and embolden our faith?

Intelligent faith is that God-connected faith that significantly influences our lives and our decisions. Intelligent faith gives us a view of God's will and purposes for us. It moves us into pursuing both the perceived difficult and the impossible and pushes us into the realm of miracles.

Intelligent faith is that God-connected faith that significantly influences our lives and our decisions. Intelligent faith gives us a view of God's will and purposes for us.

Look at the man who brought his son to Jesus in Mark chapter 9 in the Bible. He first brought his sick son to Jesus' disciples, who were unable to heal him. Later, the man shared his need with Jesus Himself. In verse 22, the man said to Jesus "If you can do anything, have compassion on us and help us."

Jesus' response was quite interesting, as was the response of the man whose child was sick. Notice that Jesus makes the object of this request the man and not Himself. "And Jesus said to him, '"If you can"! All things are possible for one who believes" (9:23). Read it again. His response does not say "I can." It says, '"If you can"! All things are possible for one who believes." Immediately the father of the child cried out and said, 'I believe; help my unbelief!'" (9:24).

Unfortunately, that internal unbelief is where many believers live today. Proverbs introduces us to a man who had memorized the right Scripture-based doctrine, but had very little intelligent, Scripture-based faith. Listen to him in Proverbs 30:4–6 and examine how accurate his doctrine of God was.

> Who has ascended to heaven and come
> down? Who has gathered the wind in his
> fists? Who has wrapped up the waters in a
> garment? Who has established all the ends of
> the earth? What is his name, and what is his

son's name? Surely you know! Every word of
God proves true; he is a shield to those who
take refuge in him. Do not add to his words,
lest he rebuke you and you be found a liar.

Now look at his self-image and lack of faith, as seen in his
declaration in verses 1–3:

I am weary, O God; I am weary, O God, and
worn out. Surely I am too stupid to be a man.
I have not the understanding of a man. I have
not learned wisdom, nor have I knowledge of
the Holy One.

Now, look at his prayer (v. 7–9):

Two things I ask of you; deny them not to me
before I die: Remove far from me falsehood
and lying; give me neither poverty nor riches;
feed me with the food that is convenient for
me, lest I be full and deny you and say, "Who
is the Lord?" or lest I be poor and steal and
profane the name of my God.

With so perfect a theology and doctrine, how do we
understand this man's low self-image and his prayer? To what
extent do you feel he internalized his doctrine so that it would
generate faith and positively impact his life? When you add
his self-image to his mindset as expressed in his prayer, how
do you think he would function had he been your father, your

spouse, your brother, or your pastor? Did having the right doctrine produce intelligent working faith in this man?

Sometimes our beliefs and doctrines do not fully filter down into our subconscious. Belief, as we understand it, is simply informational in nature. Only when it is severely tried, tested, and proved can it become faith. Belief and doctrine without pursuing the experiences they support are unsafe foundation stones for one's life.

> *Sometimes our beliefs and doctrines do not fully filter down into our subconscious.*

Faith in God helps you discover God's many gifts and blessings He ordained for you when He created you and placed you in this world. Faith opens the door to God's inexhaustible storehouse and enables you to take possession of your birthright and the dominion for which you were created.

Faith gives us overcoming power by constantly reminding us that failure is not our final destination. Failure can expand our capacity for handling pain as well as humble us and bring us a new and powerful perspective. Failure forces us to listen and understand that all life is a battlefield where we both lose and win and where God blesses us with unique and powerful opportunities to start again.

When Judas left the communion table in the upper room and went out to betray Jesus for thirty pieces of silver, he was convinced that was the end of Jesus (Mark 14;10). So certain was he that he made it the end of his own life. However, Jesus' death on the cross was the starting point to a new life of resurrection. His resurrection is what enabled the angels and the women to share the greatest news the world has ever heard. "He is not here, for he has risen, as he said" (Matt. 28:6).

What seemed like failure was not final. People who are constantly focusing on and keeping notes on their failures leave no room on the page for their eventual success.

What seemed like failure was not final.

Mary's faith in Jesus went far beyond beliefs and doctrine. It was based on personal knowledge acquired through the testing ground at the school of personal experience. If real power comes from God, the Source of all power, then you and I must move beyond simply acquiring information about God to developing deep and transforming experiences with Him. It is experiences that create true knowledge. Learning to experience God is the true "drinking of the cup" or "losing one's life to find it again" that Jesus spoke about in Matthew 20:22 and 10:39.

Mary's faith in Jesus was based on her many life-changing experiences with God as we see in the following:

- The angel Gabriel's visitation and announcement to Mary of her conceiving and giving birth to Jesus, who would be the son of the Most High (Luke 1:26–36).
- The angel's announcement to Mary of the blessing of Elizabeth with a son whom she would bring forth in her old age (Luke 1:36–37).
- Mary's faith response to the angel's announcement. "And Mary said, 'Behold, I am the servant of the

Lord; let it be to me according to your word.' And the angel departed from her" (Luke 1:38).

- The angel's special visitation to Joseph. "But as he considered these things, behold, an angel of the Lord appeared to him in a dream, saying, 'Joseph, son of David, do not fear to take Mary as your wife, for that which is conceived in her is from the Holy Spirit'" (Matt. 1:20).
- The great news the angels delivered to the shepherds in the fields about the birth of the Savior (Luke 2:9).
- The visitation and gifts of the wise men who came from the East to see Jesus (Luke 2:11).
- God's protection and provision for Mary, Joseph and Jesus while they hid in Egypt (Matt. 2:13).
- Mary and Joseph finding Jesus in the temple conferring with the lawyers and doctors when he was just twelve years old (Luke 2:42).

These were some of the personal and internalized experiences with God which formed the quality of Mary's faith. They gave her an accurate vision of Jesus, His mission and His supernatural potential. At that wedding, in that moment, and in the presence of that need, Mary was the only person with the faith to see the divine opportunity and to push Jesus into His hour.

At that wedding, in that moment, and in the presence of that need, Mary was the only person with the faith to see the divine opportunity.

How God Trained Moses
to Develop Intelligent Faith

In Exodus chapters 3 and 4, Moses is seen at Horeb, the mountain of God, tending the flock of his father-in-law Jethro, who was also the priest of Midian. While there, an angel of the Lord appears to him in a flame of fire from the midst of a bush. Two things are now present, an angel and a bush that continues to burn. We would think that the curiosity of Moses would be aroused by the presence of the angel, but instead, he looks past the angel and steps aside to see why the burning bush is not being consumed.

At that moment God now calls him by name from the midst of the bush and he answers "Here I am" (Exodus 3:4). God introduces himself to Moses as the God of his father, and of Abraham, Isaac, and Jacob. Moses falls on his face in fear. God indicates that he is aware of the oppression of his people in Egypt and the sorrows inflicted upon them by their taskmasters. As a result, He Himself has come down to deliver them.

Imagine the further surprise Moses gets when God selects him to go and confront Pharaoh with the demand to let God's people go! Naturally, Moses questions his own adequacy for such a task, but he is assured that God will be with him. As part of this assurance, God identifies Himself as "I AM WHO I AM" (Exodus 3:14). Moses is instructed to gather all of the elders as well as the children of Israel and to introduce himself as having been sent to them by the Lord and God of their fathers, the God of Abraham, Isaac, and Jacob to deliver them from Pharaoh's bondage and into a land that flows with milk and honey.

It is possible that God desired to or could have spoken to Moses through the angel from heaven that appeared to him rather than through the burning bush. In the passage, Moses apparently has seen both the angel and the burning bush, but he turns aside and passes the angel simply to see why the bush was not burning up. Interestingly, God spoke to him through the burning bush. God can and will speak to you and me, wherever we may be looking or focusing.

> *God can and will speak to you and me,*
> *wherever we may be looking or focusing.*

God then indicates that this assignment will involve tremendous challenges and difficulties, with opposition and resistance by Pharaoh and his forces. However, Moses is assured and told to have utter confidence of one thing, that God is with him. Moses then raises a reasonable question about how he would convince the people that God was with him. God's response reveals some new, fascinating, and convincing steps in developing a risk-taking and intelligent faith.

> The LORD said to him, "What is that in your hand?" He said, "A staff." And he said, "Throw it on the ground." So he threw it on the ground, and it became a serpent, and Moses ran from it. But the LORD said to Moses, "Put out your hand and catch it by the tail"—so he put out his hand and caught it, and it became a staff in his hand—"that they may believe

that the LORD, the God of their fathers, the
God of Abraham, the God of Isaac, and the
God of Jacob, has appeared to you." Again,
the LORD said to him, "Put your hand inside
your cloak." And he put his hand inside his
cloak, and when he took it out, behold, his
hand was leprous like snow. Then God said,
"Put your hand back inside your cloak." So he
put his hand back inside his cloak, and when
he took it out, behold, it was restored like the
rest of his flesh. "If they will not believe you,"
God said, "or listen to the first sign, they may
believe the latter sign. If they will not believe
even these two signs or listen to your voice,
you shall take some water from the Nile and
pour it on the dry ground, and the water that
you shall take from the Nile will become
blood on the dry ground." (Exodus 4:2–9)

Imagine being told, "Pick up the serpent by its tail"! I
wonder how long it took Moses to process that instruction.
Would that have sounded like God to you? Wow! This is not a
simple instruction but a rather tremendous challenge of faith.
I am sure that it was only after some hesitation that Moses
reached down, picked up the serpent, and experienced the
second miracle. That alone would have convinced me that I
can take God at his word.

However, God knew Moses' faith needed some more
stretching. So God gave a new directive to Moses: "Put your
hand inside your cloak." Moses obeyed. When he took his

hand out from his cloak, it was leprous. God then instructed him to put his hand in his coat again. This time, when he took it out it was totally healed and restored. If that were you, based on a scale of 1 to 10, what number would you assign to your faith level following the healing?

Faith that Leads to Miracles, Faith that Leads to Death

Hebrews 11 deals with faith and begins with an important definition of the subject: "Now faith is the assurance of things hoped for, the conviction of things not seen" (11:1). Many patriarchs are identified for their numerous exploits of faith. The chapter ends with a summary of those who died because of their faith and their absolute confidence in God's faithfulness. It also affirms that through faith, many who died are still speaking.

Hebrews 11 deals with faith and begins with an important definition of the subject: "Now faith is the assurance of things hoped for, the conviction of things not seen."

Look at what versus 32 to 38 says:

> And what more shall I say? For time would fail me to tell of Gideon, Barak, Samson, Jephthah, of David and Samuel and the

prophets— who through faith conquered kingdoms, enforced justice, obtained promises, stopped the mouths of lions, quenched the power of fire, escaped the edge of the sword, were made strong out of weakness, became mighty in war, put foreign armies to flight. Women received back their dead by resurrection. Some were tortured, refusing to accept release, so that they might rise again to a better life. Others suffered mocking and flogging, and even chains and imprisonment. They were stoned, they were sawn in two, and they were killed with the sword. They went about in skins of sheep and goats, destitute, afflicted, mistreated—of whom the world was not worthy—wandering about in deserts and mountains, and in dens and caves of the earth.

Frederick William Faber of England was a noted English hymn writer and theologian. In his best-known work, the hymn "Faith of Our Fathers" (1849), he captured the idea of a quality of faith that is needed for both living and dying.

> Faith of our Fathers! living still
> In spite of dungeon, fire, and sword:
> Oh, how our hearts beat high with joy
> Whene'er we hear that glorious word.
> Faith of our Fathers! Holy Faith!
> We will be true to thee till death.

Our Fathers, chained in prisons dark,
Were still in heart and conscience free:
How sweet would be their children's fate,
If they, like them, could die for thee!
Faith of our Fathers! Holy Faith!
We will be true to thee till death.

Faith of our Fathers! we will love
Both friend and foe in all our strife:
And preach thee too, as love knows how
By kindly words and virtuous life:
Faith of our Fathers! Holy Faith!
We will be true to thee till death.[25]

Wisdom for Living

1. Explain the idea of how every divine vision forces us to address a level of faith.
2. What divine principle did Pharaoh discover when the snakes of all of his magicians and wise men were eaten up by Aaron's rod?
3. Describe and discuss the reasons why faith without works is dead.
4. How would you explain this statement: "Faith is the main key to all possibilities. It unlocks the store house of God's universe"?
5. Hebrews 11:6 states, "For without faith it is impossible to please God." What would've been the main difference if it had said, "For without faith it is difficult to serve God"?

6. Do you remember the man in Mark 9 who brought his sick son to Jesus' disciples and then to Jesus? The man pleaded, "Jesus, if you can do anything, have compassion on us and help us." Jesus' replied, "Not if *I* can, but if *you* can believe. All things are possible for one who believes." What principle was Jesus giving to him and to us today?

Chapter 25

Your Vision Requires a Spirit of Spiritual Violence

All our dreams can come true if we only have the courage to pursue them. Faith is the radar that sees through the fog.

—Corrie ten Boom

Corrie ten Boom was a Dutch watchmaker and Christian who, along with her father and other family members, helped many Jews escape the Nazi Holocaust during World War II by hiding them in a secret room in her home. She was imprisoned for her actions. Her very famous book is *The Hiding Place*.

Many years ago, my wife and I had the special privilege of having Corrie ten Boom in our church and in our home. This was organized by Rev. and Mrs. Donald Fredlund, who served on the staff of Christian Literature Crusade and in one of the ministries of our church. Of course, everyone was thrilled and excited about Corrie's visit and ministry to us.

In that service, both she and her message touched our hearts. She spoke of the importance of forgiveness and how it is connected to our spiritual growth. She shared how, after some personal struggle, God enabled her to move from bitterness to forgiveness and finally to be able to forgive the officer who was responsible for the death of her mother and her sister. Her forgiveness was so complete that, some time later, she was even able to shake the officer's hand.

I was and continue to be impressed with how she developed her working faith. Faith is something she did. She believed God, trusted God, took risks for God, and lived out that faith to the end.

What Do You Mean by "Violent Faith"?

Were you perhaps a bit concerned about the title of this chapter, and my use of the word "violence" in relation to faith? Violent faith refers to a desperate, persistent, unstoppable, unintimidated, and God-inspired pursuit of the naturally impossible. You may ask, is there such a concept as "a spirit of violent faith" in the Bible? The answer is yes. Let's take a look at how this concept is illustrated in Scripture.

The Bible reveals four dimensions of a violent faith.

You may ask, is there such a concept as "a spirit of violent faith" in the Bible?

1. **Developing a committed, stubborn and violent faith is required if, like Elisha, we want to receive the "double portion" and the "hard thing."**

In 2 Kings 2:1–10, God is about to take the prophet Elijah to heaven and his faithful servant, Elisha, is following him with a clear request, need, and expectation. Elijah must travel to a number of cities: Gilgal, Bethel, Jericho, and Jordan. Each time Elijah tells his servant to return and not follow him, but Elisha is focused and follows him steadfastly.

Finally, after they cross the River Jordan, Elijah says to Elisha,

> "Ask what I shall do for you, before I am taken from you." And Elisha said, "Please let there be a double portion of your spirit on me." To this Elijah responded, "You have asked a hard thing; yet, if you see me as I am being taken from you, it shall be so for you, but if you do not see me, it shall not be so." (2:9–10)

Every hard thing has hard conditions and requires the paying of a high price. I have a question for you: Why do you think so many people tend to settle and become satisfied with the little things when it's possible to ask God for a hard thing and receive it?

I was thirteen years old when I asked God to help me become a pastor who had a church with a lot of land where children could play. At age twenty-two, I was reminded of this prayer when I saw a group of children playing on a large piece of land that belonged to a church. My request to God had not changed, and I still believed I would one day have it.

In 1968, I became the pastor of a church in Philadelphia, and in 1971, I presented a vision to the church that involved the possibility of acquiring a city block of land. Many in the church were stunned, and one person remarked, "This is the exact vision that was given to our church by the founding pastor in the early 1950s."

In 1982, the New Covenant Church of Philadelphia was established, and about ten years later we began looking around for additional land for a larger sanctuary and adequate play space for children. Our board of elders, my wife, and I looked for land in many locations throughout the city. There were many periods of frustration; in some instances, some of our tentative plans leaked out and spread disappointment and discouragement when they came to naught. As a result of this, one Sunday I told the congregation that we would no longer give them any progress report on the land search until we had a purchase document signed and the ink on the documents was dry.

Some months later, and after much prayer, behind-the-scenes maneuvering, and negotiations, I was able to come to the pulpit on a Sunday morning and announce that we indeed had a purchase document. It was signed, and the ink was dry. That piece of paper represented the purchase of our present campus, located on almost forty acres of land in Philadelphia. The obstacles and challenges were many, but aggressive, risk-taking and violent faith won the day.

*The obstacles and challenges were
many, but aggressive, risk-taking
and violent faith won the day.*

David wrote of God, "You prepare a table for me in the presence of my enemies" (Psalm 23:5). God does not prepare our blessings and gifts in secret, but out in the open. In light of this, have you considered that, in many instances, your enemies are more aware of your "table" than you are? Most of the time, they see the blessings coming before you do, and they begin to attack even before you are conscious of where the attacks are coming from, and why. Sometimes, just taking the time to reflect on the attacks of your enemies will give you a clear indication of where your special blessings and gifts are located.

To a certain extent, this requires, as Corrie ten Boom expressed it, "faith that sees through the fog."

2. **Developing a committed, stubborn and violent faith requires us to make some big, challenging decisions.**

Consider the decisions I have had to make as part of my life journey:

- I was put out of my home at the age of fourteen. It was very hard for me to accept this decision.
- With very little money, I struggled through four years of Bible college, but I still purposed to tithe consistently.
- When I got married in Philadelphia in 1967, due to limited resources, I had to take my bride on our honeymoon to Tennessee on a Greyhound bus.

- Several years later, we used all of our savings to help finance the beginning of our new congregation. This was a very hard decision for my wife and me.
- Later on, we decided to sell our home to help purchase the campus of New Covenant Church of Philadelphia. This was an extremely hard decision for our entire family.

If you really want the double portion, you have to give up the single portion as well as the single-portion mentality. You also have to make hard decisions.

3. A committed, stubborn and violent faith is the type that "takes spiritual things by force."

This is how Jesus expressed it in Matthew 11:11–12: "Truly, I say to you, among those born of women there has arisen no one greater than John the Baptist. Yet the one who is least in the kingdom of heaven is greater than he. From the days of John the Baptist until now the kingdom of heaven has suffered violence, and the violent take it by force."

This is a very difficult statement on the part of Jesus. "The kingdom of heaven has suffered violence, and the violent take it by force." Luke has this saying in another form (Luke 16:16): "The Law and the Prophets were until John; since then the good news of the kingdom of God is preached, and everyone forces his way into it." The King James version of Matthew 11:12 says everyone enters the kingdom violently.

It is clear that at some time Jesus said something in which violence and the Kingdom were connected. Certainly Luke and Matthew understood it, but in different ways. Luke says that every man storms his way into the kingdom. The kingdom of heaven and the miracles that God allows us to experience are not for the timid and uncertain but for the desperate.

The kingdom of God and the significant supernatural encounters that accompany it are only open to those who are prepared to make as great an effort to get into it as people struggle to survive when they feel they are drowning. It is no wonder that Jesus brings the discussion on the kingdom suffering violence to an end with the appeal, "He who has ears to hear, let him hear"(Matt. 11:15).

4. **A committed, stubborn, and violent faith recognizes that there are two forces connected to every vision: spiritual forces of opportunities and demonic forces or adversaries.**

In First Corinthians 16:8–9, the apostle Paul says, "But I will stay in Ephesus until Pentecost, for a wide door for effective work has opened to me, and there are many adversaries." Every vision, project, mission, or undertaking has giant-like adversaries positioned there to confront you. Your adversary surrounds you with influences, situations and individuals whose only agenda is to block you at every turn. David, the great visionary, also became the world's greatest giant-killer.

Every vision, project, mission, or undertaking has giant-like adversaries positioned there to confront you.

There are internal giants, and there are external ones. Both need to be identified and destroyed. Many of the biggest giants that will confront you and seek to block your accomplishments and your turning water into wine are resident within you. In seeking to identify and defeat your adversaries, don't just look for the nine-foot-tall Philistines[26] who might be threatening to defeat you or trying to shame you into nonactivity and retreat. Look also for the ugly giants in your own heart and mind—giants of fear, lack of forgiveness, resentment, pride, self-righteousness, and all of the other internal struggles that can pour poisonous water on your sacrifice instead of the fire of God.

Wisdom for Living

1. Why do you think so many people tend to settle and become satisfied with the little things when it's possible to ask God for a hard thing and to receive it?

2. Elijah said unto Elisha, "Ask what I shall do for you, before I am taken from you." And Elisha said, "Please let there be a double portion of your spirit on me." Why do you think he asked for a double portion, and what type of mindset does that suggest?

3. Elijah responded, "You have asked for a hard thing: however, if you see me when I am taken from you, it will be given to you." What price did this demand and what specifically was required for its success? What are some of the internal/inner giants that continue to confront you and impact your success?

Chapter 26

How the Anointed Staff of Moses Became a Serpent

A number of years ago, I was attending a conference with leaders from a variety of different countries, and we were discussing some rather critical issues. The chairman opened the floor for comments and observations that would contribute to the discussion. Several persons stood up and made very meaningful contributions. Then, in keeping with order, I stood and began to speak. "Mr. Chairman, I think . . ."

Immediately, the chairman jumped to his feet and said, "Shut up and sit down!" I, along with everyone else, was shocked and surprised. This was unbelievable!

At that moment I had two options. I knew I had the right to speak. I also had what I thought was a unique and

meaningful insight to share, which would have been benefi-
cial to the entire international organization. How was I going
to respond in this situation?

I choose that moment, as difficult as it was, to control my
old nature, to *not* demand my right to speak in a democratic
setting. I quietly sat down. I had been publicly insulted and
humiliated, I had lost the opportunity to speak and share my
insights, but I had not lost the battle.

Choosing not to respond negatively in such situations is,
unfortunately, not as common among believers as it should
be. My wife and I find that the longer we live and interact
with people, the more we see how quickly many people tend
to expose their negative side. For some reason, many people
feel that they cannot help it, that they have to "be themselves."

After serving and working with people since the age of
eleven, in ministries to children, youth, young adults, and
even older adults, I think there is a tremendous need for us
to take a deeper look at and catch a clearer understanding of
Exodus 4:1–5. This passage shows us that choices always have
to be made between the staff and snake.

This passage shows us that
choices always have to be made
between the staff and snake.

Moses was in the wilderness taking care of his father-in-
law's flock when he saw a great fire in the bushes and noticed
that the bushes were not being consumed. He stepped aside
to see what this meant, and the Lord spoke to him, identified

Himself, and gave him an assignment to deliver God's people from bondage in Egypt. After much doubting, debating, and clarifying, God leads Moses into a life-changing experience.

> Moses answered God, "What if they do not believe me or listen to me and say, 'The Lord did not appear to you'?" Then the LORD said to him, "What is that in your hand?" "A staff," he replied. The LORD said, "Throw it on the ground." Moses threw it on the ground and it became a snake, and he ran from it. Then the LORD said to him, "Reach out your hand and take it by the tail." So Moses reached out and took hold of the snake and it turned back into a staff in his hand. "This," said the LORD, "is so that they may believe that the LORD, the God of their fathers—the God of Abraham, the God of Isaac and the God of Jacob—has appeared to you." (Exodus 4:1-5, NIV)

Wow! Moses' mind is blown! He never understood or realized that there was or could be a "snake" in his staff. Even though his staff reflects the anointing of God on him, the snake represents the fall of man and is a touch of the curse through sin. There is a snake in every person, and both the manifestation of the anointing as well as the snake can emerge in every natural thing, including your career, your natural strength, talents and ministry.

Salvation brings the staff of anointing to all of us. Yet our old sin nature leaves a snake in all of us. It is our responsibility to control the snake and allow the anointing—the staff, representing the wisdom, self-control, and grace of God—to abound.

Picking up snakes by their tails is a very important part of the process that leads to success. Let us take a look again at God's interaction with Moses.

In Exodus 4, God had given Moses a mind-boggling and faith-stretching assignment. This was one of God's ways of extending the capacity of Moses for the significant task God had for him. God's next step was to get Moses to exercise his faith, so he changed Moses' staff into a snake—big enough and frightening enough that Moses ran from it. So what does the Lord command him to do next? "Pick up that snake by the tail."

"Pick up that snake by the tail."

Pick Up the Snake by the Tail

Common sense says, No! All of our past experiences say, No! Our survival instincts say, No! Our education says, No! Our friends and family say, No! People with religious experience say, No! Can you imagine would have happened to Moses, to the rest of the Israelites, and to us, if Moses had said No?

Fortunately, he did not. Instead, Moses put forth his hand and caught the snake by the tail. It took considerable faith for him to obey God's command. His actions demonstrate that true faith and obedience drive away fear and conquer all difficulties.

We must be aware that every divine vision or call has a number of serpents in it. Let us look at Exodus 7:8–12 to see how Aaron, Moses' brother, handled his serpent experience:

> The LORD said to Moses and Aaron,
> "When Pharaoh says to you, 'Prove
> yourselves by working a miracle,' then you
> shall say to Aaron, 'Take your staff and
> cast it down before Pharaoh, that it may
> become a serpent.'" So Moses and Aaron
> went to Pharaoh and did just as the LORD
> commanded. Aaron cast down his staff before
> Pharaoh and his servants, and it became
> a serpent. Then Pharaoh summoned the
> wise men and the sorcerers, and they, the
> magicians of Egypt, also did the same by their
> secret arts. For each man cast down his staff,
> and they became serpents. But Aaron's staff
> swallowed up their staffs. Still Pharaoh's heart
> was hardened, and he would not listen to
> them, as the LORD had said.

Can you possibly read and internalize this and not get excited about God?

Note how Moses instructed Aaron to throw his rod down, just as God had earlier instructed him in the wilderness. Moses had learned a significant faith-stretching and miracle-making lesson, which positioned him to encourage Aaron to test his faith and to experience the miracle-making capacity of God.

Moses had learned a significant faith-stretching and miracle-making lesson.

The message is very clear. Your anointing for the impossible and your table of blessings are always prepared and presented to you in the very presence of your enemies, including the serpents.

The Snake We Pick Up Can Become the Rod of God in Our Hands

Dietrich Bonhoeffer (February 4, 1906–April 9, 1945) was a German Lutheran pastor, theologian, dissident anti-Nazi, and founding member of the Confessing Church. His writings on Christianity's role in the secular world have become widely influential, and many can be found his book *The Cost of Discipleship*, a modern classic.[27]

Apart from his theological writings, Bonhoeffer became known for his staunch resistance to the Nazi dictatorship. He strongly opposed Hitler's euthanasia program and genocidal persecution of the Jews. He was also involved in plans by members of the German Military Intelligence Office to assassinate Adolf Hitler. He was arrested in April 1943 by the Gestapo and executed by hanging on April 1945 while imprisoned at a Nazi concentration camp, just twenty-three days before the German surrender. One of the many things for which he is remembered is this statement, a summary of his understanding of his faith: "When God calls a man, He bids him come and die."

This statement directed Bonhoeffer's life and reminds me of a story I read when I was a teenager—a story that helped to galvanize my faith, my trust and my confidence in God. It's the story of the forty wrestlers.

Forty Famous Wrestlers[28]

A Roman legion was encamped in the dead of winter on the shores of an Armenian lake. The sun had gone down, and night was falling when the soldiers were drawn up in line to hear the imperial edict ordering all men in every place, on pain of death, to pour a libation before the image of the Emperor, in token that they acknowledged the ancient gods of Rome.

It was a strange scene: the flaring torches, the ranks of men with set, stern faces, the officers standing near the rude altar, the ensigns of Rome fluttering in the bitter wind, and beyond these the dark and terrible lake on which, if any refused to obey, he would be sent naked to meet his death in the long winter night.

One by one the soldiers filed past the image of the Caesar and poured out the libation.

But now, a soldier, young, stalwart, straight, stepped out of the line and with high uplifted face said, "I owe no allegiance before that to my Master, Christ," and stood aside. The line filed past and another and another stepped out until there stood together forty soldiers, so strong, so daring in every deed of courage or feat or arms that they were called by their comrades the "Forty Famous Wrestlers."

The Roman general stood aghast, "What is this?" he cried. "Do you understand what awaits you there?" He pointed to the lake. "A dreadful death to wander there the long night through because you will not pour a few drops of wine before the image of the Caesar. You need not believe in the gods of Rome. I do not believe in them myself, but surely your Christ does not require this of you, and do you think I am going to lose my forty best soldiers for such a whim? Tomorrow at evening the ranks will form again. If you obey, well; if not—the frozen lake. Throw not your lives away."

I do not believe in them myself, but surely your Christ does not require this of you

They were young, the forty wrestlers, and life was sweet. Each heart held the thought of home, a little home amidst clustering vines and olive trees where father, mother, wife, and children waited for them. Life was sweet and death upon the lake was cruel and the pouring of the libation a little thing. Would the Christ care?

The short winter day was drawing to a close as the legion formed in line. Again the torches flared, and the eagles of Rome looked down upon the solemn scene. No word was spoken as the soldiers filed silently past, pouring the libation. But when the first wrestler's turn came he stepped quietly out, and the light upon his face was not that of the fitful torches, but the light of the other world.

Taking off his helmet, he laid it at the feet of the general with his sword and his spear and shield. On them he laid his cloak, his tunic, and his warm, close-fitting undergarment, then turned to the lake, singing in a clear, sweet voice as he went to his death:

Forty wrestlers wrestling for Thee, O Christ,
Claim for Thee the victory and from Thee the crown.

The second followed, and his comrades, dumb with wonder, watched him lay down the arms he had so gallantly borne, lay down his garments and his life, and go on the dark and gloomy lake of death singing, too: "Forty wrestlers wrestling for Thee, O Christ, Claim for Thee the victory and from Thee the crown."

Another and another followed till all the forty soldiers were out upon the lake and forty voices had taken up the triumph song. Slowly the night wore on, and the guard in the house on the bank where warmth, clothing, food, and drink were waiting for any who might turn back, heard the song grow fainter and more faint as one by one the voices failed. At last, just at dawn, one wrestler came creeping back, but even as he lifted his hand to deny his Lord he fell lifeless.

Then the guard, who could not bear that the band should be broken, took off his helmet, and laying down his shield and spear and garments, went out to join them, singing exultingly "Forty wrestlers wrestling for Thee, O Christ, Claim for Thee the victory and from Thee the crown."

Dietrich Bonhoeffer was right. "When God calls a man, He bids him come and die."

Wisdom for Living

1. Why is the ability to pick up snakes by their tails such an important demonstration of faith?
2. Why is there always a clash between true faith and common sense?

3. What do you think is meant by the statement, "We must be aware that every divine vision or call has a number of serpents in it"?

4. What did Dietrich Bonhoeffer, the German Lutheran pastor and theologian, mean when he said, "When God calls a man, he bids him come and die"?

Chapter 27

Capture Your Mission
and Do It

In 1980, my wife and I were sharing ideas with our friend the Rev. Birtral Beard of Trinidad. He and his wife were very effective in ministry and impacted the lives of thousands of individuals. Suddenly, he asked me a penetrating question that required much thought: "What do you sense God is doing and wants to do in your life?"

I began to think, then shared aspects of my vision at the time. His reply was stunning, and I have never forgotten it to this day. He said, "It would be a great shame for both of you to go to your graves without giving birth to your vision." From that point on I made it my number one priority to capture and to do my mission. I determined that I would do my level best to ensure that the statement never came to pass.

In John 18:37, Pilate asked Jesus a question. "Then Pilate said to him, 'So you are a king?' Jesus answered, 'You say that I am a king. For this purpose I was born and for this purpose I have come into the world—to bear witness to the truth. Everyone who is of the truth listens to my voice.'" In his book *Man's Search for Meaning* Viktor Frankl, a professor of psychiatry and neurology at the University of Vienna and president of the Austrian Medical Society for Psychotherapy said, "Everyone has his own specific vocation or mission in life. Everyone must carry out a concrete assignment that demands fulfillment. Therein he cannot be replaced, nor can his life be repeated. Thus everyone's task is as unique as his specific opportunity to implement it."

Jesus lived His entire life executing this principle. It is exactly what his response to Pilate's question expresses. In a very succinct and unabashed way, Jesus communicates to Pilate and all those listening that He was the King, the promised Messiah.

At the beginning of this book, I mentioned that from my earliest recollection, I was convinced that I wanted to be "a fitherman like Peter." Everyone around me and all the members of my family understood (even though I couldn't pronounce the word correctly) that I meant I wanted to be a "fisherman." My sense of call and mission was clear long before I came to experience Jesus Christ as my Savior.

My sense of call and mission was clear long before I came to experience Jesus Christ as my Savior.

My experience in the Church of God with missionary pastor Herman Smith, his invitation for me to become his helper, his demonstration of forgiveness after I had a fight in VBS, and later his allowing me to teach a Sunday School class when I was eleven-and-a-half years old all contributed to solidifying what my mission was going to be and the church through which it would take place.

The way in which the Rev. Smith and his wife connected with me reminds me to some extent of the story in First Kings 19:19–21, where Elijah the master prophet found and called young Elisha. When Elijah saw the young Elisha, he felt led to transfer his mantle of anointing on him, and immediately something happened. A supernatural connection was established and a destiny was imprinted. The Bible says, "Then he arose and went after Elijah and assisted him" (1 Kings 19:21). The New King James versions says, "then Elisha left and followed Elijah, becoming his servant."

As a young man, Elisha was faithfully serving his family in simplicity and obscurity by taking care of oxen. Likewise my daily chore as a child was to take care of goats. While the young Elisha receives no mention thereafter until Master Prophet Elijah was old and about be taken up to heaven (see 2 Kings 2:1), I, on the other hand, was allowed to move into the ministry of serving at our church long before I became a teenager.

What was young Elisha seeking with such diligence, consistency, and determination? He was seeking his vision, which was to receive a double portion of his master's anointing. Note, not simply a similar anointing, but a double portion of it. Knowing what God wants for you in this life is one thing. Being willing and committed to pay the price for it is another.

As I interacted with my pastors, I developed a keener sense of God's calling on my life. It is this sense of divine calling that helped me withstand the ridicule from friends and family (and especially from my school friends, who called me "the white man's slave"), from the professor who tried to make me feel that having a mind of my own was a bad thing, and finally from colleagues who could not stand to see where God was taking me and has brought my wife and me.

> *As I interacted with my pastors, I developed a keener sense of God's calling on my life.*

The Philippian church was the first Christian church in Europe, and Lydia, who sold purple linen, was part of the major leadership. Actually, the church met in her house. In Philippians 2:12–13, the apostle Paul shares a principle with that congregation. He wrote, "Therefore, my beloved, as you have always obeyed, so now, not only as in my presence but much more in my absence, work out your own salvation with fear and trembling, for it is God who works in you, both to will and to work for his good pleasure."

We don't get the full impact of the verses when you read them in the English Bible because the translation of that passage robs us of the impact of the message. If you were studying Latin or Greek for instance, you would learn that the laws of Latin are different from the laws of English; they instruct us to put the predicate in a different place in the sentence and the subject in another. They call for the articulation of the principle first, and the implication second.

To really understand what Paul was saying in these two verses, you have to rotate them. You have to put verse 13 before verse 12, which helps on see the cause first and then the effect. As such, the two verses would read as follows: "for it is God who works in you, both to will and to work for his good pleasure. Therefore, my beloved, as you have always obeyed, so now, not only as in my presence but much more in my absence, work out your own salvation with fear and trembling."

What Paul was saying to the church of Philippi was that God was planting or working a powerful and life impacting vision and mission inside of them. The imagery behind the concept of "God . . . works in you" is *impregnating*. God was impregnating the church in the way the Holy Spirit impregnated Mary and caused the Word to become flesh. In the same way, we should understand that he has already impregnated us with a divinely designed vision. It is He who is overshadowing us and is saying to you as He said to Mary, "That which is to be born of you shall be of the Holy Ghost."

Divine impregnation with a life-changing vision is always a three-part process. First, God plants a vision in your inner spirit. He then equips you with the will to do it. Finally, He empowers you with the ability to work it out through fear and trembling. The ability never fully manifests itself until it knows that the will to do it is in place. Then God gives you the capacity to become the person that the vision and mission actually create.

From the foundation of the world God determined your package. If you are a child of God, you have been empowered

From the foundation of the world
God determined your package.

with divine genes. The Spirit of God who caused Christ to become flesh in the person of Jesus, now communicates God's mind so that you can fulfill God's purpose for your life. It is in this way that His kingdom comes and His will is done on earth as it is in heaven.

There will always be people who try to convince you that it cannot be done. Mary was very wise. When the Holy Spirit impregnated her, she didn't go to Joseph to explain to him how it happened. He would never have understood. The Bible says that right after the angel spoke to Mary, she went to the hill country to visit with Elizabeth. Why did Mary not go to Joseph but to Elizabeth instead? It is because Elizabeth was also pregnant. She was experiencing the same thing; she understood. Actually, when Joseph did find out, he contemplated putting her away privately. When God impregnates you with a vision, you have to be very careful not to tell it to the wrong people.

Let's go back to Philippians 2:12. "Therefore, my beloved, as you have always obeyed, so now, not only as in my presence but much more in my absence, work out your own salvation with fear and trembling." This means total dependence on the One who placed it in you.

A number of years ago, many people were convinced that my wife's and my shared vision was impossible. Many said, "If you leave Philadelphia and go to another state, your vision might work, but you've been ministering in this city for fifteen years. You can't resign a great pastorate, then go twelve blocks away and make that type of vision happen. It just wouldn't work." Time has proven that a major part of our vision was fulfilled because we have been committed to working it out.

God allowed Mary to push Jesus to turn water into wine. The capacity to do it was already deposited in Him. She pushed Him to work it out. How did He do it? He took a risk of faith by instructing the servants to fill the water pots with water.

I believe that God heals, but if I don't lay hands on the sick person as a pastor and believer, I don't give God a chance to do it. Faith is giving God a chance to prove Himself. The faith that puts God on the spot gives Him an opportunity to prove Himself. It is God working in you, causing you to do what is right, to expand your thinking, to explore some possibilities you've never explored before, to think bigger than you've ever thought. God's job is to work it in. Your task is to believe and to work it out and see it happen.

> *Faith is giving God a chance*
> *to prove Himself.*

When a woman is about to give birth the doctor says, "Push!" All life comes through pushing, and all growth and success come through pushing. We push hard into things that are significant. If you are really pregnant with a vision, sooner or later you will feel it kicking and building up in your spirit. It won't let you rest. You'll sense it and feel it. You will be taken over by it, and you will do it. You will do it because that is what true vision from God does: it pushes you and releases in you the ability to turn your bitter water into wine.

The choice is squarely yours: you can choose to live in the quagmire of bitter water, or you can choose to live your life experiencing the miraculous process of those waters being turned into wine. If you have not yet made the decision to do the latter, I invite you to make it. If you have made the decision as I did, I encourage you to tell your story as I have told mine. Let us start a movement that gives people hope just as Jesus did.

Wisdom for Living

1. How do you explain this statement? "When a woman is about to give birth, the doctor says, 'Push!' All life, growth and success come through pushing."

2. How would you explain this principle to an individual? "Work out your own salvation with fear and trembling, for it is God who works in you, both to will and to do his good pleasure" (Phil. 2:12–13).

3. When Mary became pregnant with Jesus, why did she go all the way to the hill country to find and tell Elizabeth instead of telling Joseph?

4. What vision has God impregnated you with that you need to bring forth?

Notes

Chapter 1

1 You will notice that throughout this book I refer to the Rev. and Mrs. Smith interchangeably as Brother or Pastor Smith and Mrs. or Sister Smith. It was common practice in the Caribbean when speaking about them to call them Rev. or Pastor and Mrs. Smith, but when addressing them directly to call them Brother and Sister Smith.

2 East Berbice-Corentyne is one of the ten regions in Guyana covering the whole east of the country. It borders the Atlantic Ocean to the North.

3 Georgetown is Guyana's capital, on South America's North Atlantic coast. Culturally connected to the English-speaking Caribbean and located in the Demerara-Mahaica region, it is the country's largest urban center.

Chapter 2

4 Guest was an English-born American poet who became known as the "People's Poet." From his first published work in the Detroit Free Press until his death in 1959, Guest penned some 11,000 poems, which were syndicated in some 300 newspapers and collected in more than 20 books.

5 Edgar A. Guest, *Collected Verse of Edgar Guest* (NY: Buccaneer Books, 1976), 599.

Chapter 3

[6] Read 1 Samuel 17 for the full story on David and Goliath.

[7] Todd Smith (personal blog, 2010) http://www.littlethingsmatter.com/blog/2010/06/25/the-power-of-personal-initiative/.

[8] Todd Smith (personal blog, 2010) http://www.littlethingsmatter.com/blog/2010/06/25/the-power-of-personal-initiative/.

Chapter 4

[9] http://www.hymntime.com/tch/htm/j/i/m/jimcross.htm.

Chapter 5

[10] http://www.beliefnet.com/quotes/angel/a/albert-einstein/there-are-only-two-ways-to-live-your-life-one-is.aspx.

[11] Jesus is fully God and fully man. In light of this, we can talk of Mary "pushing" Jesus into a new aspect of ministry, but we recognize that Jesus did not do anything He didn't want to do, or anything that was out of God's will.

Chapter 6

[12] According to https:///hymnal.org/ there is no biographical information available on Fidellia H. Dewitt.

[13] Theodore Geisel (Dr. Seuss), *I Can Read with My Eyes Shut* (Penguin Random House, 1978).

Chapter 11

[14] Robert Loveman (1864–1923), "April Rain" (poem).

Chapter 12

[15] https://www.britannica.com/biography/Herod-Agrippa-I.

[16] Flavius Josephus, born between AD 37and AD 38 in Jerusalem. He was a Jewish priest, scholar, and historian.

Chapter 13

[17] http://www.onespiritinterfaith.org/2013/08/august-6-2013-desmond-tutu/.

Chapter 17

[18] Brickdam is the area located to the east of the Georgetown, Guyana's capital city. Brickdam is the single most concentrated area of Executive departments and agencies.

[19] https://www.umcdiscipleship.org/resources/history-of-hymns-jesus-keep-me-near-the-cross.

[20] https://hymnary.org/text/whether_i_live_or_die_whether_i_wake_or_.

Chapter 20

[21] Lisa Matthews, "What Is a Wolf Personality Like?" http://wolfsongalaska.org/chorus/node/20.

Chapter 21

[22] Hans Christian Andersen, "The Emperor's New Clothes," in *Fairy Tales For Children*, First Collection (C.A. Reitzel, 1837).

[23] Paul's missionary journey to Rome is chronicled in Acts 27.

Chapter 22

[24] http://www.stempublishing.com/hymns/biographies/cowper.html.

Chapter 24

[25] http://library.timelesstruths.org/music/Faith_of_Our_Fathers/.

Chapter 25

[26] First Samuel 17 tells the story of how David defeated Goliath, the nine-foot-tall Philistine.

Chapter 26

27   Deitrich Bonhoeffer, *The Cost of Discipleship* (Touchstone, 1995).

28   http://www.otteryreformed.freeola.net/40famous.htm. From The Reformer (official organ of the Protestant Alliance), May/June 1992. Used with permission. Copyright © 2000, Ottery St. Mary Reformed Church.